Memoirs of a smoker, laryngectomee and public speaker.

A Silver Lining Story

George Willets

With Peter Wright and Deborah Peel

iUniverse, Inc.
New York Bloomington

"That's Easy For You To Say"
Memoirs of a smoker, laryngectomee and public speaker.

iUniverse books may be ordered through booksellers or by contacting:

iUniverse
1663 Liberty Drive
Bloomington, IN 47403
www.iuniverse.com
1-800-Authors (1-800-288-4677)

ISBN: 978-1-4502-3037-7 (pbk)
ISBN: 978-1-4502-3038-4 (ebook)

Printed in the United States of America

iUniverse rev. date: 6/4/10

Chapter I

Awakening

Surfacing from morphine's sweet stupor, my first rational thought was where am I?

I couldn't figure out what the bright lights and blurred gray shadows were. Were they ghosts? Was I dead? A sharp upper body pain answered my question, and I remembered – and wished I were dead. A nearby alarm went off — beep-beep-beep. I went to turn it off but I couldn't move my arms. Within seconds blessed relief arrived; the sweet unguent of morphine again dulled my brain into peaceful submission.

*

That dazed awakening came after more than ten hours on the operating table. Ten hours of intricate, perilous surgery in order to remove irreparably damaged tissue, to save my life: self-inflicted damage I had willfully wreaked upon myself over the past fifty-one years.

I drifted in and out of consciousness for a week, my brain anesthetized by morphine. During lighter moments I figured that this had to be the highest high of my life, but stabs of pain brought me back to reality. Sometimes when I came to the room was full of light; at other times there was nothing but gray. But my perception of time was counted in the number and frequency of shots of pain killer. I thought that I had bottomed out years ago when I had swapped the bottle for the twelve step program, but when they started to reduce my morphine dose, the reality that excruciating pain was my life became clear. I had found a new bottom.

Physically, I thought that I was at the end of my tether: strapped to a hospital bed, unable to move my arms, and wires connecting me to a bank of monitors against the walls like a group of overseers recording my every flinch. Intravenous tubes snaked from my limbs, a feeding tube ran up my chest and through my nose, and I could sense rather than feel, bandaging around my left thigh and right shoulder. They both burned relentlessly. What else had they done? My upper chest and neck seemed buried in miles of gauze; now, that made sense.

Like Death Valley during the summer, I suffered a craving thirst. To make matters worse I was unable to utter a sound and call for water. They had immobilized my head, limiting my world to views dead ahead. I tried to resign myself to simply closing my eyes and shutting it out. My throat, however, screamed incessant white-hot pain, like a thousand needles being jabbed into my skin from the outside, being turned around and drawn back out over and over again. The only merciful relief came in the form of morphine.

But my drug induced euphoria gradually turned against me and produced nightmares filled with hideous monsters and demons. Nothing I could do at that time would remove those images. They lurked everywhere behind my eyelids. And then, paradox of paradoxes, the addict in me begged for a cigarette. *Just ONE!* To be inserted between my parched lips so that I could inhale an evil blast of hot poisoned smoke to soothe the savage craving.

Chapter II

The Hubcap Gang

Summertime in Orange County can bring hot days and warm nights. We boys from Fullerton used to cruise in my immaculate Chevy, windows down, looking for "thrills." There were five of us: Joe, Ronnie, Bob, Squeak and me; we called ourselves the Hubcap Gang. We weren't bad boys, you understand, but boys from hardworking families living respectably in good neighborhoods. Cruising the streets, we would whistle at the girls and exchange racy remarks, and when things became too dull, we'd steal hubcaps. It was southern California in the 1950's and it was all about the adrenaline rush.

Joe and I were from fairly well-off homes, well Joe more than I. We lacked for nothing. The rest of the gang came from working class families. Some might ask what we thought we were up to roaming the streets on any given night of the week? Others, with more savvy, would expound that no matter the youth's upbringing, where he came from, there is a period in life when the hormones are active and the spirit is restless. From about sixteen to twenty, a touch too much freedom and limited discipline allowed us to roam the streets seeking the big reward – the adrenaline rush.

I was the driver – the getaway man. I loved to cruise the streets looking for action — anything! While nonchalantly meandering down one of the main drags, one arm hanging out of the window, the other gently directing my car, I'd often wonder if the pedestrians looked at me admiringly – cool, man! Too dark to do any more girl-watching, I would mark the territory, cut the lights and pull in behind an Oldsmobile to pursue our other activity – stealing hubcaps.

"Can you get 'em?" I whispered loudly behind me, "They're flipper hubs." A minute later, Joe was back clutching the prize which he stashed in the trunk.

"Woo-hoo! We did it!" We yelled, congratulating each other.

"Man, one more second and I'd have been nailed." Joe was exultant.

"We're invincible," I assured the others, flashing a big grin at my buddies in the back seat. That's when I saw it - oh-oh! was that a police car?

Making sure that I didn't exceed the speed limit, I took off across the next intersection.

"Joe said, "There's a cop car right behind us." Sure enough, there it was – with lights flashing. It let out one *whoop* of its siren; I pulled over.

After the usual preliminaries, the cop explained that a passing driver had reported a Chevy, like ours, engaged in some kind of activity a block and a half back up the street, and would I now please step out of the car and open the trunk?

There they were, spread out across the bottom of the trunk; booty in the form of assorted hubcaps from previous nights of thrill-seeking adventure. We were all booked into juvenile hall. We lingered there for seven days. In that unfamiliar, hostile environment, it might as well have been seven years.

My father had died a year before, a blow that had inadvertently released me from firm paternal control and given me more freedom. It was my mother who tearfully, unbelievingly came to visit me. After an hour of futile "how did it? and "why did it?" questions, she tearfully decided that the whole thing was a terrible mistake. The other guys also were visited by their parents, some of whom, I fear, were not so lightly dismissed. Joe's father hired a lawyer who acted on behalf of all of us, and steered us through the legal proceedings. He also convinced the judge that we were no threat to society and should be released to our parents care – with a period of probation.

The seven days in juvenile detention and subsequent sentencing had drawn us five boys together: made us a real gang! Home, for me, was a place to get out of the rain and a place to sleep. It was dull and boring. We had never been a close knit family and since my father's death, my mom had isolated. I needed to be needed and my four buddies were those I looked up to and from whom I wanted acceptance. Low self-esteem had always been an anchor around my neck. I wanted to feel special. My companions filled that emptiness inside me.

Now that the Hubcap Gang had been so ignominiously disbanded, the probation period became an opportunity to make plans – to dream of more adventures – and I leaped at the chance.

Chapter III

Do Not Disturb - Nightmare

Random thoughts crowded my mind; like a swarm of yellow jackets in a bottle. Memories of our hubcap adventures and priceless times with the boys made my face twitch into the beginnings of a smile. The resultant facial pull on stitches sent a message to my brain which screamed in agony. My face was a mask of raw pain held firm by antiseptic tape and tubes. It hadn't occurred to me that my head had to stay immobile in order to be remotely comfortable.

Darker reflections, faster and more intrusive than those that attempted to make me smile, created waves of remorse interspersed with feelings of worthlessness – emptiness.

What had I done to deserve this? Why me? Of one thing I was certain, sweet morphine would bring peace to this troubled mind.

What terrible thing had happened to me? One minute I was a carefree sixteen-year-old, the next I was engulfed in pain and self-loathing. During a moment of clarity, I remember the doctor telling me that I would probably live. Another dark shadow overtook my senses and I wondered if that was a good thing. The doctors hadn't told me precisely what they had done. How much had they carved me up? Vanity emotionally outstripped gratitude.

The ICU nurse was at my bedside again. "How are you George?" she cheerfully piped as she removed some of the surgical coverings to do what she had to do. I knew what was coming and instinctively winced to help ward off the pain. Like an injured animal I withdrew from human contact to protect myself.

I counted each dressing as the nurse gently removed it. It felt as though she was using a steam shovel and I gripped the bed rails until I could grip no more, my strength completely ebbed. Gone was the smooth leg I had owned for fifty-odd years. What appeared to me in its place was a flayed limb: a large piece of proud flesh was missing.

My gentle administrator then turned her attention to my neck which had suffered an equally cruel bite. That part of my anatomy which had been cut and carved for access to the cause of all this butchery, had been deftly patched with the other part of my body; a lovely skin graft.

A sponge bath came next. From the carnal cells in my brain, temporarily out of action, came a message reminding me that under different circumstances, the intimate ministrations of this gentle lady might be pleasurable. I experienced discomfort with every swab and every wrinkle of my skin.

My gentle minister finished her merciful duties on my wreck of a body and proceeded to fulfill her duties as a humanitarian by adjusting my morphine drip. Before fading to oblivion, I watched her behind switch out the door and on to her next victim.

Chapter IV

1313 Orange Grove Lane - First Drags

The aromatic smell of oranges pressed in on us as we darted through the grove of trees. Carefully spaced, endless rows of citrus were heavy with fruit and the leafy canopy shut out the sunlight pressing down overhead. This orchard lay amid the urban sprawl where we lived. Where the sidewalk ended, so began this secret territory; it seemed to call our names.

I lived on Princeton Avenue in a respectable new house with my parents. My buddy Norman and his family lived in a huge colonial style house bordering the large orange grove. My dad was a house painter; Norman's dad was mayor of Fullerton. Apart from two spirited boys about the same age, the other commonality we shared was the brand of cigarettes our dads bought by the carton. At age eleven, I remember the thrill I got after lifting a pack from dad's carton; like stealing the Hope Diamond.

Our stash was at 1313 – thirteen trees down from our entry spot and thirteen trees in, carefully hidden in a crutch of small branches at arms height. Norman got there first and reached up to retrieve the prize. Quite often wind and weather, and occasionally small wildlife, would ruin a pack of smokes, but today it was unblemished. He produced it with a triumphant flourish, "Yes!"

We crouched expectantly at the base of the tree while I produced matches and Norman shook a few pungent Pall Malls half out of the pack.

"Don't mind if I do," I said in my best Humphrey Bogart. I clamped the cigarette between my lips and got it lit. Norman eagerly grabbed the matches and did the same, but sucked too hard on his first drag. Chest exploding, tears streaming from his eyes, he tried to cover up his immature attempt at worldliness.

I, on the other hand, had been quick to pick up the technique from my dad, and drew in a short puff, exhaled it and dreamily watched the gray smoke drift away.

Grinning, I asked Norman, "Do ya feel it?" I looked at his freckled face and saw only puffed red cheeks and tears. "I guess so," he wheezed.

We both laughed and fell on the grass. I felt the tobacco tweaking my young brain and liked it. Giggling, I rolled over and propped myself on one elbow tried to emulate Bogie by holding my cigarette languidly between two fingers.

We were big shots now. Equally impressed with each other's foray into grown-up land, we could posture, practice our street slang and tell outrageous stories knowing that our secret was safe here among the orange trees; they knew it was okay for us men to have a quiet smoke in the afternoon – they wouldn't let on.

"Norman . . ." A distant mother's voice called. Then slightly louder, "Norman . . . time to come in."

"Oh, shoot," Norman scrambled to his feet and grabbed the Pall Malls. He crammed the pack back in 1313 where we hoped to find it undamaged on the next date in the orange grove.

We each dug a small hole in the dirt and covered up our butts.

"I'm coming," yelled Norman, as we began to make our way back through the trees to the exit hole. As we trotted under the low lying foliage, we each grabbed a handful of the bright, fragrant leaves and began to chew them hoping to disguise our breath.

At eleven years of age, we had no fear of sucking poisoned smoke into our unspoiled lungs, only a fear of getting caught – and innocence is no protection.

Chapter V

Coming Around – Introduction to Reality

"Hey buddy," a familiar voice pulled me back from the orange groves of my boyhood. I raised heavy, unwilling eyelids to a new day. I looked to the left and realized that they had removed the restraints from my head. I could now turn my entire head without damaging my neck.

The man sitting in the chair next to my bed leaned forward and I made out a ruddy face and tousled hair: it was Skip, a newly sober friend whom I had been sponsoring. I started to form the words to greet him – but nothing happened.

"It's me – Skip!"

I blinked my eyes to acknowledge I knew he was there and knew what he said. I was almost happy to see him but was nonplussed both by my restricted movements and inability to speak. I wanted to offer my hand. I was supposed to be supporting him. Seeing it flutter on the bed, he reached over and covered it with his.

"Just wanted to make sure you weren't alone," said Skip. "I understand you're going to make it. I've been sitting here off and on for the past three days."

I closed my eyes hard and Skip squeezed my hand. I offered a gentle squeeze in return.

"Some other guy named Dave has been here too. Do you know who I mean?" he asked.

I shrugged my left shoulder and shook my head slowly, deliberately no.

"Black guy named Dave. He had surgery like you."

I closed my eyes hard indicating that I understood. It had to be Dave from Denny's, I thought. What in the world had he been doing sitting in my hospital room? I never expected that. Pretty nice.

One of those daytime soaps was airing on TV. I really wanted to switch channels. My mind began to wander. My own life seemed like a soap opera. Twice married, children I barely knew anymore, and a lucrative car-striping business down the tubes. I threw it all away in favor of fast living and far too much drinking. Nine years sober, now, I lay helpless in ICU. Wishing to change the TV channel would not keep the soap opera from playing and replaying in my mind.

I fumbled for a notepad and pencil, my only real means of communication. Thus far my attempts to write notes to the doctors and nurses had been a clumsy failure. Through the fog of my anguished mind I wanted so much to connect, but my thoughts, too complicated to write, didn't make it down the chute. This time, however, I managed to write T and V.

Skip got it right away, grabbed the remote control and started scrolling down the channels.

"Tell me when to stop – oh, sorry!" Skip's face flushed with embarrassment when he remembered my condition. He eventually found CNN, and I moved my hand. How bleak it sounded, news from all over the world coming to an unhappy man in a hospital bed.

Wryly I thought of the situation. Here was Skip sitting by my side offering support without reservation or conditions. Well, maybe one. Who would want to lose his AA sponsor when he was just about to receive his sixth-month chip? In spite of my respect and love for the guy, I could hardly wait for him to leave. Nobody needed to see me like this.

As he turned to go I looked up at him again and saw in the pocket of his white shirt the familiar rectangle of a pack of smokes. An outraged energy gave me enough strength to reach up and grab the pack. A startled Skip gave an "oh" of surprise as I crushed them. That was the last day that he smoked. He was able to quit without employing the morphine technique I was obliged to use. Some small miracles do occur from time to time.

Skip saw the doctor coming and stood to leave. "Hang in there buddy," he said and smiled as he walked away. I gave a mental sigh of relief as Dr. Rice, clipboard in hand, pulled up a stool and sat down beside me. I concluded, after all, that visitors were a luxury I didn't really need.

"Glad to see you awake and more alert today, George," said Dr. Rice. I closed my eyes firmly in a nod.

"This looks like a good chance to bring you up to date on your condition." He waited a minute, looking at his notes before continuing. "Even though you may feel as though you have been hit by a bus, George, everything is going pretty much according to routine. Dr. Petty and I agree that the surgery went very well, although it presented a few challenges. It took a little longer than anticipated." I listened intently as he continued. "I want to assure you that we removed all the cancerous tissue. You aren't going to die – at least not from this." He paused and I knew he expected me to smile – yeah, right! "We found a very large tumor in your throat which we were able to remove. However, we did locate other suspicious tissue and had to biopsy and test as we found it. This extended the procedure well beyond the estimated four hours; you were actually in surgery for ten hours." I mouthed "whoa" at him. "And, George, in addition to the tumor in your throat, we were forced to remove your vocal cords. We knew beforehand that the cancer was well advanced. The laryngectomy, however, was very successful. You are just on the brink of a lengthy recovery and it's going to be one step at a time from here on."

My eyes welled with tears. I squeezed my eyelids tight but the tears ran down my cheeks. I had begged God to make me well, or take me out. I didn't think He'd go that far.

Just hearing the word 'laryngectomy' shattered my ego. I realized that I was still clutching the notepad and managed to scratch out a message for Dr. Rice.

He took the notepad and answered my question. "Without your vocal cords you will never be able to speak like you did in the past. But that doesn't mean that you won't be able to communicate. We'll look at all the options a little later on in your recovery. For now, I'd like you to concentrate on the positive – you are certainly going to live, and you are going to feel a heck of a lot better than you have for a long time."

Dr. Rice squeezed my good shoulder gently as he closed his chart. He had warned me as we had prepared for surgery just how bad it might be. He had even indicated a worst-case scenario of having to remove my breast plate. That had really got my attention.

Subconsciously I knew things could have been a lot worse, but a loud voice kept yelling "You can't speak!" How does one measure out gratitude?

I heard the doctor's footsteps retreat down the corridor; my savior off to save some other poor soul. If, as the good doctor had said, I'd felt as though a bus had hit me, now I truly felt as though I'd encountered a steamroller – just call me Wile E. Coyote! Doom and gloom! I was certainly going to live, the man said, but what kind of life would that be?

I had never before felt so entirely alone.

To make matters worse, an enthusiastic nurse arrived shortly after Dr. Rice left. Would I ever get a break? But there was one big reward. I no longer felt the needle sliding into my hip — dreamland here I come.

Chapter VI

Cigar Central

I impatiently watched Squeak as he ceremoniously broke out the cigars and solemnly handed them around to the boys lounging about my bedroom floor; like a ritual. Crook's cigars were a special brand: soaked in rum for extra flavor. Recalling the high I'd experienced sucking on cigarettes in the orange grove, it didn't take long before I, too, was a happy recipient. Unfamiliar with cigar-smoking, I assumed they must surely be bigger and, therefore, better.

My bedroom was in an add-on at the back of the house with its own private entrance. We were all teens. Saturday night was here and tonight was going to be the most excitement I'd seen for quite some time. After the hubcap bust, part of the terms of my probation was that I be home by 8 o'clock each night. At age sixteen that was a fate worse than death.

Squeak, the officiate, offered initial instruction on preparing the cigars and we all made a big show of getting them fired up with quick little puffs.

"Hey, what about your mom?" asked Bob.

"Ah, don't worry about her," I said, "She hardly ever comes back here. Even if she does, what is she going to do? Call the police?"

Everyone burst out laughing while I basked in the attention. I turned the volume up on the radio and opened the window to let some of the dense haze in my room drift out into the cool of the evening. What if my mom did smell the cigars, I thought, she wouldn't say much. I knew her too well. Her approach to life was peace at any price, and that was why she left me alone. I was king in my little room at the back of Princeton Avenue. For the rest of that summer, my room became Cigar Central.

"D'you think we'll all get drunk from the rum?" I hollered, remembering my first drunk the year before when I was fifteen. I got a lovely buzz from Country Club Malt Liquor. After the first couple of gulps, I found a new George inside me – a George just like all the other guys. Maybe even better, a super guy! We'd all sat on the hill overlooking Fullerton and got plastered. We never made it down to the railroad tracks to Joe's house. We drank too much and got sick.

A similar sense of freedom and well-being came over me as I dragged deeply on that Crook's cigar. A little too deeply! Smoke poured down my nose – and I coughed.

"You don't inhale cigar smoke," scolded Squeak.

"Yeah, you don't inhale," echoed the rest of the guys, appearing to know all about cigar smoking.

"Well, I thought I'd get more rum or something," I glumly replied.

Inhaling was a shock to my system. After that I got wise and let the smoke linger in my mouth but never pulled it deep into my lungs. Intent on getting the hang of smoking, I pursued it like a profession, until it became an easy painless habit. Like everything else in my life I gave it 110 percent of my attention and effort. I had to show the guys I could do it better than any of them.

One evening, Squeak brought a new brand of cigar, Hava-Tampa. Just as we were about to start playing cards and light up the cigars, a knock on the door brought the room to its feet. It was my mom.

Squeak, who had already lit up, tamped out his sleek, swanky cigar. The others hastily hid their unlit smokes and I opened the door.

Rather than rant and rave about under-age boys smoking and ruining their health, and how she was going to tell all the parents, Mom held out a plate of cookies. "I thought you boys might like something to eat," she chirped.

"Thanks Mom," I said grabbing the plate of freshly baked chocolate chip cookies.

"Hi, Mrs. Willets," sang Squeak over my shoulder.

"Hi, Squeak, hi boys," she called back, but turned away looking somewhat confused. With a little half wave she left.

I closed the door and turned to the guys feeling rather uncomfortable. "See, I told you she wouldn't bother us."

We munched down the cookies and smoked all the cigars. It was another summer night hanging out at my place; another day of lost innocence.

Chapter VII

Little Hershey's Kisses

I clearly remembered the bragadaccio of those summer smoking sessions. I felt the love while I shared the poison bond of smoke with my buddies. Those early days were sharp in my mind as I moved from the critical area of the ICU to the 'you're gonna make it' area of the same ward. Valentine's Day was just around the corner – ironically to be one of my more memorable lover's days.

My new room symbolized progress in my immediate recovery. It looked very much like the other ICU place, perhaps a little sunnier. The same measly eight TV channels greeted me, but my flights into space were winding down as they weaned me off morphine. I was being stepped down and harsh reality was beginning to jar its way into my tranquility.

The first visitor in my new room was Dr. Rice. He had continued to provide me with more details of the operation and the surgical blueprint of my reconstructed throat. He also directed the nursing staff on how to reduce my pain medications, including morphine, so that total dependency didn't result.

I could no longer speak, and the manner in which I breathed and swallowed food had been changed to accommodate the empty spaces created by the removal of tissue and not-so-proud flesh. Now I was able to understand what that cold explosion was when my liquid lunch was poured into my feeding tube. The feeding tube entered through my nose, down my esophagus to my stomach, and that's where my lunch arrived in a big splash.

I had another pipe that almost followed the same route, but to my lungs. Dr. Rice explained the need for a very uncomfortable steel rod sticking out of the stoma at the base of my throat. The nickel-sized hole was my airway, the only way to get oxygen into my lungs. My nose and mouth no longer provided these services – they were just facial decorations. I was told that the steel canula might have to stay there for months, at least until the raw flesh had healed.

That was as much good news as I could take that day. Dr. Rice took his leave.

Valentine's Day rolled around with a visit from my current girlfriend, Jeannie. She had arrived on my scene shortly before my surgery. Unlike my usual lean and mean, no nonsense type of girl, I loved her plentiful curves and especially loved the way she held my hand, even more so when I told her about the diagnosis of cancer and the resultant surgery – a laryngectomy. Here she was at my bedside with Valentine treats. She was offering Hershey's Kisses to a man with no throat surviving on liquid lunches!

My "to hell with it" attitude came to the fore – I was going to have one of those kisses. What if I got her to shave off the tiniest slivers of chocolate . . .? Yes! I would place just a sliver on my tongue and wait with patient restraint as it melted and trickled, drop by drop, to my stomach. I wondered about the wisdom of this rebellious move. Might it be fatal? Could I die by choking? Perhaps it was because Jeannie was there, but my machismo took the lead. Somehow I didn't care anymore. I was a man, I reminded myself, and I was going to indulge in a little Valentine's Day lovefest.

I managed to persuade Jeannie to remove the bright red wrapper from the chocolate and hand it to me. With some hesitation, she placed the chocolate kiss in my hand, and I, ceremoniously, placed it on my tongue. As to the planned little slivers melting and running down my throat – there were none, just the smooth outline of one beautiful kiss. My taste buds jumped to attention, ready to fulfill their duty to me.

To my surprise, only the faintest flavor of chocolate became evident. But after too many liquid lunches, even the weak taste of that delectable sweet was heavenly.

The kiss didn't go down smoothly as originally planned, but I dared not cough. It might have destroyed the surgeon's handiwork. I think perhaps I meditated it down.

Jeannie stayed about an hour before leaving to set up the condo I had rented where we would live after I got out of the hospital.

When Dr. Rice visited me that evening, I pointed out the gift basket and the chocolates. I scribbled on a pad and passed the note to the good doctor. It said, "Ate one."

He was not amused. Even though I wrote as much as I could about how careful I was and my idea that only the melted chocolate would be swallowed, he continued to scold me, telling me in no uncertain words how foolish and selfish such a trick was. It was he that had the last laugh – he confiscated my gift basket.

My morbid sense of humor provided me with a good night grin. Had I died as a result of my foolish adventure, the newspaper headlines may have blared: **Man Defies Cancer: Death by Chocolate.**

Chapter VIII

Marlboro Red Box

Prior to my hospital admission, I'd spent several years going to AA meetings, attempting to recover from alcoholism. One of the AA maxims, One Day at a Time, kept racing through my brain while I lay recovering in the ICU step-down unit. All I had for entertainment were the eight lousy channels, not much of a distraction. It dawned on me that I was powerless over EVERYTHING. Control was a dream of the past. I was just there, at the whim of a string of doctors and nurses on duty day and night to provide sufficient medical care and attention to heal my physical body. Yet they dispensed no potions or pills or medical procedures to heal my emotional and mental condition. It eventually became clear that job would be up to me with, as AA recommended, God's help.

Lying in a hospital bed staring up at the ceiling was a good place to think – to ponder.

It became the order of every day for me to recall some of the highlights of my life before this recent operation. The tinny TV voices and the piped in laughter aggravated the misery in which I now soaked.

There were the days when I was a real scrapper. I played high school football, basketball, was on the swim team, and even played a trumpet in the band. There was no stopping me. I believed in myself.

Perhaps it was the big screen TV that spoiled me, entertaining myself with other people's stories; their hardships, their victories and their defeats. Watching sports was one of my favorite pastimes. I had a voice and used it to holler at the players. All of my youth and vigor had evaporated and reappeared as a breathless, middle-aged guy lounging about on the sofa smoking Marlboro's. Smoking, smoking, and sitting on the sidelines.

People thought it sort of cute when my voice became husky. I guess I did too. You could quite confidently have said that I was a committed smoker. I had smoked Marlboro red box for thirty years. I had tried to quit, but it always seemed that it wouldn't quit me.

I was totally addicted to nicotine, that toxic alkaloid in cigarettes. I couldn't be bothered that it was also used in insecticide. The addictive habit, now a compulsion, had hold of my brain, my lungs and my heart – and my right arm lifting endless cigarettes to my mouth. Every morning the first thought in my head was, "*this* is the day I give it up." I wrestled fiercely with my common sense but never won. I just rolled over and lit up and immediately felt utterly disgusted with myself.

One winter I developed a nasty cold. The infection went right through the family: my girlfriend, Anne, and her two daughters. At the height of the infection we all had scratchy voices and coughs that wracked the body to the core. After a few days, however, the other three in the household began to improve. I did not. My cough got so bad that I thought that my lung would appear one day. My voice eventually disappeared beneath layers of mucous and pain. Did I quit smoking? Oh, no! Not for one minute did I stop lighting up and stubbing them out. Everyone else got their voices back. Not me.

During the time it took for my voice to show signs of re-emergence, I sat in front of the TV surfing – and smoking. Dumb? Certainly, but not to me. I was sure that just plain old cigarettes couldn't be affecting my throat. No way. It was the damned infection and nothing else.

Finally, I could whisper well enough for people to hear me. My voice had come back.

Revisiting that period of my past life brought me to the stark realization that I had brought on my own misery. Images of cartons and packs of Marlboro cigarettes haunted me, taunted me.

I did get my voice back after that cold, albeit not the voice I once had, but enough to ignore its weakness. Maybe if I'd looked after myself I may not have lost it forever. The next cold I caught resulted in the same thing. Only this time my throat began to ache all the time. My whole body began to ache. My denial gave way to common sense and I dragged myself to the doctor's office on leaden legs.

Chapter IX

Diagnosis

I went to see my family doctor first. Before looking at the place that was bothering me, he gave me a routine examination to make sure I was otherwise healthy. I knew something was seriously wrong with my throat, so with some dread, I opened my mouth as wide as I could while he examined as much as he could see of my throat and larynx. He asked the obvious questions; Did I smoke? Did I drink? I told him "yes" to both, but hastened to add that I'd quit drinking three years prior and was now sober.

"Well, George," he announced, "it doesn't look good. I'd like you to see a specialist, an ENT man. I'm not an expert, but it looks to me as though you may have a tumor affecting your vocal cords and that has affected the volume of your voice." I nodded. Then he delivered the whopper. "There may also be cancer present."

Hearing the 'C' word was like hearing a judge sentence me to death. My little world fell apart and I became truly afraid.

The doctor wrote my referral out on a slip of paper which I took to his receptionist. Instead of giving me the name and number of the ENT, she picked up the phone and dialed him directly. He had an office not too far away. Anne was with me and said she'd drive me right over. Frightened to death, but with eternal hope rising in my breast, I thought that maybe my physician was wrong. He wasn't an expert. The tarnished hope lasted another fifteen or so minutes.

"How long have you been smoking, George?"

"Since I was a kid, I guess. At least thirty years."

"Drinking?"

Pulling my hand out of the cookie jar, I proudly told the specialist, "Sober three years." And that I was a member of Alcoholics Anonymous – all to no avail.

"You have a large tumor down there, George, and it may be malignant. It's affecting your speech. I'm afraid it's got to go. First thing you have to do is stop smoking."

"You mean today?" I asked.

"Now," he affirmed. It all sounded so matter-of-fact coming from him. I'm sure he knew I had throat cancer as soon as he glanced down my throat. Drinking and smoking are two of the recreational pastimes no vigilant doctor would condone.

This doctor certainly seemed to know his stuff. He was talking and I, still in shock, barely heard him until the word "options" came booming through.

"We'll get you into the hospital as soon as possible and biopsy that tumor. If it turns out to be malignant, we might consider treating it with chemo and radiation. But your tumor is so big and so badly placed, that I believe I'd recommend surgery."

Anne had become alarmed at the severity of both the diagnosis and the treatment, but I needed her to see me through the next phase of my life. Unhappily our relationship at the moment was not exactly serene. Although she was the most current in my series of amorous adventures, we had been having our ups and downs for some time. Now I desperately needed her comforting hand to hold.

The following day I checked into the hospital where they prepped me for the biopsy. Hours after the removal of a slice of the affected part of my throat, I came to. The first thing I felt was a deep, stinging pain in my throat, worse than I had ever experienced. They had already attacked the enemy by slicing into it and my body was rebelling as only it knew how. Every muscle in my body ached like the worst attack of influenza multiplied by ten.

The results of the biopsy confirmed the ENT's prediction – cancer.

Now that Anne and I shared the anticipation, dangers, and resultant consequences of surgery, our personal life together became less turbulent. I realized she was interested in more than a brief thrill. My usual way of dealing with serious threats to my personal freedom, that is to say when the time came to consider a more solid relationship, I became lukewarm. Then I'd cut and run. With this in mind, I shared my thoughts and fears of the diagnosis with Anne and Dr. Stewart. In essence I was terrified. How could I get cancer? Other people get cancer. My dad smoked all his life and never got the disease. Nearly everyone I knew smoked as much as I and they didn't get cancer. The hospital already had me scheduled for surgery. I felt like a lamb being led to slaughter.

Dr. Stewart listened patiently to my frightened ramblings, and asked me if I thought I was getting the best care possible. I didn't know. How could I know?

"If you were president, and you had cancer don't you think you would get the very best medical care in the country?"

"Well I'm not president," I said, "and I have no idea where to find, or how to find the best surgeon in the country." Fact of the matter was that I was just an auto pin-striper with a business that declined during my drinking days. No matter how good my skills, drinking killed my business.

"What would you say, George, if I told you that one of the leading surgeons in the world lives and practices right here in southern California?"

I didn't say anything for a minute, my mind grappling with this news and the words "options" and "second opinion." Maybe a second opinion might be different. I formed the words slowly. "How would I find this surgeon?"

Chapter X

The Second Opinion

I often pictured my dad bent over double with his hacking cough and wondered if smoking had burned his heart out? Thoughts about my own lungs and heart quickly followed and I could only conclude that they probably were in the same, if not worse shape than his. Would I, too, die like him? I had reduced my smokes to two per day, and it hurt like hell to smoke them. The mental anguish of not smoking was far worse. Unable to make myself understood on the telephone, I asked Anne if she would contact UCLA Medical Center and get through to their ENT department.

Locating Dr. Thomas Calcatera, chief head and neck surgeon, was easy. So easy that within minutes of calling and following two directives, Anne was talking to the good doctor's nurse, and I had an appointment scheduled.

Two days later I anxiously awaited the appearance of Dr. Calcatera in a sterile examining room. He arrived professionally dressed in a spotless white coat, stethoscope around his neck and spotlight strapped to his brow, followed by a retinue of young doctors, nurses and students. Like ducklings, they trailed in the wake of this tall, thin and imposing figure. He wasted no time.

Viewing my file quickly, he glanced over and asked, "Are you drinking, George?"

I vigorously shook my head, no.

"How about smoking?"

Again I shook my head, no. It has been two days since my last painful cigarette.

""Good," he said decisively, "because if you were, I wouldn't even look at you."

He made a few notations in my file, asked me to sit on the edge of the examination table and told me to open my mouth wide. Shining a brilliant lamp down into my throat he spoke to his students and explained some medical phenomena as each of them peered into my gaping maw.

"The biopsy has already shown that this is cancerous," Dr. Calcatera said pushing the light away. "What is it that you want to know?"

"What to do," I whispered. "I'm scheduled for surgery."

He glanced through my file again, had another quick look down my throat and said, "Radiation. I recommend that you seek radiation therapy. Why cut when you don't have to?" Then he was gone.

I now knew what course to take. If I were president, I would seek radiation treatment. And so I did.

Chapter XI

Radiant George — Survival No.1

Elated to think that I was going to avoid surgery and have my cancer disappear with doses of radiation, Anne and I left the hospital to celebrate at Hamburger Hamlet. Munching on a big, juicy hamburger, I hoped, maybe, I'd be back to normal in a few weeks. It had been a long time since I felt so energized.

While we were enjoying our burgers, I saw a familiar face in the booth just across from us. It was Beau Bridges drinking coffee and perusing a dog-eared script. He caught my eye and gave me a smiley-eyed grin. Seeing a famous actor right next to me and having been in close contact with a world renowned surgeon was quite something – a special day. I felt even surer of good things to come.

Getting ready for radiation would prove an intricate and exact procedure in itself. Dr. Calcatera directed me to the Loma Linda Medical Center where technicians made a mold of my face in fiberglass. Fitted with short flanges, the mask could be bolted to the table during treatments, preventing me from moving even a micro-millimeter. My neck and throat were measured and geometrically tattooed with markers to show the radiographer precisely where to zap.

For the next seven weeks, at exactly eight o'clock each morning, I journeyed to the basement of the Loma Linda Medical Center.

There, lying on a hospital table, wearing a hospital gown, they bolted me to the table with my facemask and began the procedure. The remote controlled radiator positioned over my neck directed a fifteen-second burst to each marker.

Radiation didn't make me sick, and that was good. My voice, however, slowly but surely disappeared. I also had a continuously sore throat. My unhappiness and discomfort with the medical situation was compounded by a deteriorating relationship with Anne. To complicate matters, both were affecting my business. The only source of income I had was the auto body shop where I did the pin striping and managed about seven other spot painters and detailers. Anne finally agreed to help me run the body shop when I was not feeling up to par. My crew complained about Anne's attitude toward them; they said she had no tact.

In spite of the inevitable fatigue, I headed from Loma Linda directly to my body shop every day following the complaint. At the end of the seventh week my tumor had gone – and so had Anne.

I became an official cancer survivor. I had beaten the odds and my body was intact. The only visible relic was the hard, radiated skin on my neck. The nerves in my voice box rallied and I began to whisper; then the volume increased, but the timbre was missing. Never mind: I could speak, I could be heard.

I was back to normal; another ordinary guy who'd actually beaten cancer. As the days went by life became more beautiful. Ideas of drinking and smoking began to filter into that part of my brain where my "committee" was housed. I had been sober for three years and I had seen the wreckage that alcohol can do. I'd seen men and women lying in the gutter drunk! Self respect – gone! Homes – gone! Jobs – gone! Some ended up in the insane asylum. Not for me, I thought, not for me. I'd continue to attend my AA meetings. I was going to be okay.

My committee is a pretty rational group. They told me that nobody ever lost a job because of smoking, or lay in the gutter because they smoked too much. Nobody ever ended up in the insane asylum because they smoked. I asked my committee, the sensible part of my brain, what about cancer? Well, my committee said, nobody has proved that cigarette smoke causes cancer. That's a gimmick on the part of Surgeon General to get people to stop smoking, but only because it is anti-social. Is that right? I had to agree with all that rationalization.

It didn't matter how I had started to smoke again, whether it was one-a-day for a week, or whether I smoked a whole pack in one day. The fact is, within a month I did start again – and that was enough. One cigarette was too many, and a thousand were not enough! The compulsion had not left me.

Chapter XII

The Chimera

Before I picked up a cigarette again with the intention of smoking it, I had thought about it and expressed my intentions. There may have been a handful of "friends" who agreed with my rationalization, but, by far, the majority, most prominently Dr. Calcatera, strongly advised me not to smoke then, and never to smoke again. They implied that my throat would never take the smoke again and that there was a strong possibility the cancer would recur. The trouble was that the further behind I left smoking, the stronger the neurotic compulsion became to smoke. It became an obsession. Finally, my spirit succumbed to the wants of my flesh – and I had my first cigarette since radiation. I was off again on the road to ruin.

That road led to the hospital bed where I now lay. My burning inner question became *what have they done to me? What do I look like after all the surgery?* In my younger days I was a nice looking kid. Handsome even! Now, just past fifty, I hadn't given much thought to my looks, but I'd been reasonably content with them. Asked if I looked okay, visitors, including Jeannie, had off-handedly said, "You look fine; nothing to worry about." Or "What do you think you look like? You've just had major surgery."

I'd never been able to let well enough alone, and one rainy morning my headstrong curiosity got the better of me. Feeling as weak as a kitten, I managed to get my feet on the cold hospital floor and lurch upright holding on to the IV pole. I shuffled over to the bathroom door and clutched the door frame. Eyes shut, I managed to switch the light on.

I slid in behind the bathroom door and turned to look in the mirror. *WHAT HAD THEY DONE?* I beheld, not me or anything like me, but something from a Hollywood horror scene. Filled with outrage, dread and shame, I quickly turned away. Instead of the swell of a masculine neck I had shaved many times, I saw only a carved out, crusty cavity; a crazy steel canula protruded from a hole recessed at the base of my neck. There was no Adam's apple. My neck seemed to curve inward into my chest. I had had the impression, or the distinct idea, that all the disfiguration caused by the removal of the tumor and other affected parts, would be internal. I had never suspected that the outward reconstruction would be so obvious.

Radiation, that fickle cure of nodes, warts and tumors, can also cause untold damage to healthy tissue situated close to the affected area. It tends to turn skin tissue into a substance resembling dried leather – hygroscopic and brittle. Because of the radiation treatment I'd undergone after my first diagnosis, the skin and tissue adjacent to the cancerous mass had lost its elasticity. It was no longer a useful part of my body – it couldn't be stapled or sewn.

Doctors Petty and Rice had scanned my body and selected two areas where the skin was most pliable and closely resembled the skin deleted from my neck. With infinite care, two sections were taken, one from my thigh and another where my left shoulder connected with the armpit. This skin now formed a glistening covering for the trunk of my neck.

So that was why other parts of my body bore wounds so unbearably painful when the dressings were changed. Ointments and salves generously daubed over my neck and the other raw places were maintaining the graft. What I considered to be an unholy mess was described by the doctors as "healing nicely."

I stared at the image in the mirror, shocked by what I saw. How can I meet people looking like this? Any vanity I may have had, vanished in a glance. A cancer survivor, I thought. A monstrous creation, I screamed. And created by me by smoking cigarette after cigarette for thirty years, and consuming drink after drink for about half that time. That kind of abuse might easily kill someone. It nearly killed me. In that moment, I wished it had.

Chapter XIII

First and Last

I was sixteen again and Jenny laid claim to my body. I was her handsome high school sweetheart. Wrapped in each other's arms we swore our love would last forever. We belonged to each other, mind, body and soul. Ah, sweet sixteen and the extravagant blindness of young love.

"George," cooed Jenny in that dreamy tone I came to dread. The red flags were, this time, blowing more strongly. "George, I really think we ought to get married."

"Maybe we will — someday," I said after the initial cold shock had died, and nuzzled my face into the crook of her neck in an attempt to steer her mind elsewhere.

My first sexual experience dominated all of my sixteenth year at school. All I could think about was Jenny, her body, and the feel of her skin. I daydreamed in class, missed band practice, and drove to school whenever I could expressly so that I could drive her home. My school buddies ragged me mercilessly. Joe said I'd disappeared! I didn't care. I just wanted to be with her, spend time in her pink bedroom until her parents got home just before dinner. We would undress and admire each other's bodies. Afterwards, Jenny would sigh with contentment and plan our future together. At first I didn't say anything. I didn't actually disagree but allowed my thoughts to wander . . . .

My dad died that spring. A heart attack at forty-five ended the family I had known my entire life. My dad had always been the boss in our family. He ran a tight ship and ran rough shod over the emotions, hopes and aspirations of mom and me, especially me.

However, when mom got mad at him, the seat of power changed, and, for some reason that I could never understand, he allowed his wife to have her way. If dad were the head of the family, mom was the neck turning the head. I guess I was too young to understand what marriage was all about. It seemed to me that there were no constants.

My dad had smoked as long as I could remember. I remember helping him roll his handmade cigarettes, and the way friends used to think it quite adorable to see little George help dad roll his smokes. There are home movies, somewhere, with pictures of me licking one side of the paper to hold the tobacco in. There was no Surgeon General's warning of the danger of smoking tobacco, and when dad had his massive coronary, the doctor didn't associate his death in any way with smoking.

I remember well the day my dad announced to the family that he was going to quit smoking. And quit he did – for a day! As the day wore on, he became more and more agitated and started to pace up and down outside the house. He paced until mom could stand it no longer and snapped at him. "Oh, for God's sake, just have a smoke." Tranquility returned. He didn't attempt to quit again.

Dad, a house painter by trade, was a hard, steady worker. All the paints he used were lead based, and it is probable that his death was the result of breathing a blend of paint fumes and cigarette smoke for many years. Interestingly enough he gave up his painting job because, he said, the fumes made him sick and gave him headaches. He switched roles and became a successful salesman in the paint shop.

In spite of my dad's strictness, I did respect him. I paid little attention to his condition when he became sickly and suffered lung problems because I was wrapped up with Jenny and my own secret world. I didn't watch him slowly depart this world. It seemed to me that one day he simply fell over dead.

"George. George!" That insistent reminder from Jenny interrupted my wandering thoughts.

"Jenny, Jenny," I mumbled. "I was just thinking of my dad, you know. This is really not a good time for me – for us to talk about stuff." I felt her expel all the air from her lungs against my neck and knew that she was angry. It seemed to be coming to a head. She wanted an answer. Just before my dad died, she had broken the relationship off after asking me the same question about getting married. She was giving me time to think about it. Me? I didn't give it a thought. I wheedled my way back into her arms. Where was all that love now?

We were sitting in the car parked by a playground near her house. Jenny sat bolt upright and pushed me away, leaned over and turned off the radio.

"I mean it, George," she came at me again. "We should just go and get married."

Oh, boy, I thought, she's just not going to let up. She had caught me in a moment of weakness the last time we'd had this struggle. At that time I'd have said anything just to make love to her again. Now it seemed she meant it. I reached over to retrieve my cigarette from the ashtray.

"Sue and Bob did it," she whined. "They just ran off and got married." There was an anguished silence. "They truly love each other," she went on, "and if you really loved me you'd marry me." Another brittle silence. "It would be okay. I've thought it all out."

That was the final jab. "Oh, yeah, right!" I burst out. "And how are we supposed to live? I'm not even out of high school yet!" I took a deep drag on my cigarette and glared out of the window.

"Well you could start by getting a job, work full time," she continued eager to win me over. "And I bet your mom would let us have one of her apartments across town. I could fix it up real cute – we could be so happy." Silence. "You do love me don't you?"

Angry at her idea about the apartments, I exploded, "Dad left those apartments to mom! They are her only income at the moment. She needs renters. Why can't we leave things just as they are?"

Jenny pouted sullenly, but I was too angry to allow her to speak. "What are you talking about?" I yelled, stubbing out my cigarette in frustration. "Í'm almost in my senior year; I can't get a full time job."

"Yes you could, too," she came back quickly. "You'd have to quit school, that's all – if you loved me . . . ."

"That's all," I repeated, hardly believing what I had heard, "That's all?" I couldn't imagine what she was really thinking. We were teenagers for Christ's sake. We couldn't get married. I wouldn't get married.

"I thought you loved me," Jenny cried. "I'm good enough to sleep with but not good enough to marry. Is that it?"

"I didn't say that," I said. "But this is just crazy. I'm not about to quit school to marry you. It doesn't mean I don't love you." I paused. "My dad just died and things are weird at our house. I just can't do this."

I knew what was coming next. She burst into heart breaking tears and bent over toward the dashboard. I patted her back and tried to brush the hair off her face. She slapped my hands away, while I slumped over and leaned against the door. Jenny's crying continued as I stared out of the window. I knew she was doing her best to make me cave in. Making a positive move, I turned the key in the ignition and put the car into reverse.

Startled, she sat up and cried, "What are you doing?'

"What do you think? I'm taking you home." I stayed quiet and concentrated on guiding the car toward Jenny's block. The atmosphere in the car was full of silent conflict, my mind filled with disbelief at Jenny's ultimatum. What was going on with the girl?

When I pulled in alongside her house, I left the engine running. We both just sat there staring straight ahead. Finally she turned her head and faced me. "Well?"

I tried to keep the waver out of my voice. "I told you I'm not ready to get married, but that doesn't mean . . . ."

Before I'd finished the sentence she was out of the car, flouncing her way toward the house. Then she turned on her heel and came back clutching her blue angora sweater to her throat. She looked at me through the passenger window and fixed me with a harsh glare the likes of which I'd never seen before.

"Come on, Jenny..." I despised the whine in my voice.

"We're through," she spat coldly and raced back into the house, blue angora trailing behind her. The end of that romance was echoed by the double slam of the screen door.

Jenny was my first love, and lover, and she had dumped me! I sat there for several minutes commiserating with myself. I'd never delight in that special powdery scent she had. I was devastated. My dad was gone — my girl was gone. I started to drive, and drove until late into the evening, smoking packs of Marlboro red box. Jenny was my first love and I was sure that she'd be my last.

Later, after the initial blow of loss had eased, I recognized, too, my reversal of fortune. What a near miss. She had almost had me. I wished more than anything I could just go talk to my dad.

Chapter XIV

A Hint of Silver Lining

I lay in bed that day, my face covered, awash in sad reflection. I gave Jeannie the silent treatment with no notes and asked her to leave. I couldn't face her. I couldn't face anyone. I slept fitfully, and dreamed of orange groves, and Joe and Norman, and smelled the pungent smell of oranges and nicotine smoke. Ironically, the surgery to remove my cancerous killer had deprived me of my sense of smell. It was banished to my dreams.

Lying alone, wishing to be alone, often gives rise to some strange fantasies and disturbing thoughts. The mask of the face I now bore had erased all of my thanks to God for being alive. I had forgotten all about asking Him to think kindly and not allow me to die. What strange creatures we are, I shamefacedly admitted. I had asked for salvation — and rejected the reward.

Both the doctor and the nurses knew that I'd made it to the bathroom; there was no use them trying to play down my new appearance. Dr. Rice, however, talked me through the various aspects of the grafting, and urged me to face the inevitable with all the courage I could muster. The nurses, too, cajoled me into walking the hospital corridor with my IV. One day the doctor told me that I'd be leaving pretty soon and I'd better get used to people looking at me.

Each time I saw Jeannie, I saw horror in her face. I turned away as though that would create a cure-all. What must she think of me now? Could she still love me? Did she still like me? I was quite sure that Victor Hugo's *Quasimodo* had nothing on me.

Lying in my cubicle one afternoon I heard a young, excited voice telling someone in the next bed all about a recent basketball game. My nurse came in and announced that it was a beautiful afternoon and that we should all enjoy the gorgeous sunshine. As she said this, she whisked back the dividing curtain, allowing rays of light to stretch across my bed.

I saw, it seemed for the first time, large patches of blue sky broken up with white puffy clouds. Almost simultaneously, I caught sight of the dark haired, lanky youth, still extolling the better points of the game. His youth, vigor, and a breath of life reminded me of days gone by – of Norman, Joe and Squeak. Draped over the back of a chair, he looked at me and looked away out of the window. But something had been revitalized in me. I couldn't stop looking.

Out of the corner of my eye I watched the young man continue talking vivaciously. He glanced at me from time to time, and then tentatively flashed me a smile.

He had smiled at me! It broke through my cloud cover just like the sun parting the cumulus fluff outside. A sudden change took place inside me and I knew someone had accepted me and my ugliness. At the same time I knew that my life was about as bad as it could be: breathing through a hole in my neck, unable to talk. Who on earth would ever team up with me? Well, this young man had. In his smile I had seen a new beginning. The old adage *every cloud has a silver lining* sang through my head. I knew I had to get better again.

As I allowed this epiphany to expand, I realized that I had to make a difference. I just couldn't let this pain and horror go by unnoticed. I must have a job to do. During my worst days and nights, at my weakest, riddled with pain and vomiting, I had made a deal with God. I had promised Him that if he pulled me through, I'd return the favor. Now I was about to make another deal with Him. I promised Him, and me, that after I left that hospital I would help other people, in the best way I knew how, to avoid the agony I had just endured and the humiliation I was about to go through for the rest of my life.

My thoughts focused on the smiling young man, about my age when I took a class trip to Disneyland. There I was at the happiest place on earth when I accepted my first Marlboro from a classmate, adding cigarettes to cigars to develop an addiction that would almost kill me. It had all been so avoidable, I futilely ruminated. The only hint of cancer survival's silver lining came in a single smile from a teenage basketball fan.

After four months in the hospital, I was strong enough to go home. I had no idea what I was in for, but as I drove away I knew I had faith and ambition.

Chapter XV

Regression

The new condo didn't thrill me. I'd compare my arrival in it with checking into a Travelodge rather than a cozy bed and breakfast: necessities but no charm. But give Jeannie her due, she had set it up well. Nothing was lacking. This place would do during the first stages of my recovery. The main thing was that it was close to the hospital and doctors.

That condo soon became prison-like; perhaps due to my own bull-headedness. I never asked for help. I broke hospital rules by walking to the car at my discharge. I tried refusing Jeannie's arm when entering the condo and nearly passed out. Wallowing in a well of self-pity and self-imposed frustration, I ended up sitting on the edge of the bed, head in hands, listening to Jeannie chatter about what bargains she had won with the furnishings, and did I see the big TV?

That first night at home, I learned a lesson. I woke in the middle of the night needing urgently to go to the bathroom. I started to call for Jeannie, but there was no voice, no noise. The realization of how we mortals take our voices for granted startled me. Was I simply an empty vessel? As I fumbled in the dark and knocked the lamp over, Jeannie appeared in the doorway and asked what I was trying to do. For me, it was a very humbling way to attract attention.

Nothing in this condominium was familiar. Jeannie had spent almost all the money I had fixing it up. I had given her permission, but she, nevertheless, received the brunt of my stress. She had taken a leave of absence from her job to look after me. She did her best to nurse me, trying to settle me down in bed or on the couch, and giving me my meds on time. But it didn't work. Her patience ran out and she returned to work.

Alone and depressed, the glint of silver lining I'd seen in that hospital bed vanished. In all my life, I had never felt so low, so pathetically lonely. Wandering into the garage was as close as I felt to comfortable at the condo. I would sit in my old tricked-out El Camino and dream of days gone by. The relief I felt was real but temporary. Drugged up and desperate for joy, I took it for a drive one day – just up and down the block. My El Camino was as close to home as I could feel.

Returning to the condo was never fun. It seemed that I had lost my identity; I was a non-person. I found my interest in communicating steadily waning; I realized Jeannie was not going to be part of my solution. My non-verbal presence drove her out of the house time after time, to work or elsewhere, leaving me in mental turmoil. Two weeks after I had been discharged, she told me she was moving on. I didn't really blame her.

My car became my love affair, my only home. One day, I took her for a run down the block again, then sat slouched in the driver's seat inside the garage. An unusual sense of peace and contentment came over me. I sat a while and enjoyed it. For some unknown reason, the words of a minister I once heard came back to me. He said, "Be in this world, but not of it." What did that mean to me? I think it meant that I, if nothing else, was a child of God, plain and simple, and that's all I needed to know. Somewhere I had a purpose. I just had to wait to find out what it might be. My connection, the place where I had found comfort, was my car. I'd just have to see how it all worked out.

Chapter XVI

The Robot Man

In my now silent condo, I played around with my electro-larynx, practicing to get the hang of it. I moved it around from place to place trying to find the sweet spot where I could process the vibration it created on my throat. I was very self-conscious. I'd stand in front of the mirror and try not to come off like an idiot as I worked hard to perform my robot talk.

The electro-larynx was a device that helped me verbally communicate. By holding the sensor firmly against the flesh of my throat and mouthing what I wanted to say, vibrations were transmitted through my mouth. The noise emitted, although mechanical and 'robot' sounding, was identifiable as the English language. Listeners tended to listen to the noise rather than the words. I had a love-hate relationship with my E-L, but I decided that beggars couldn't be choosers.

I finally called a couple of friends and explained the predicament I had found myself in. Jeannie had moved out, I told them, and I was left with a condo I couldn't afford – and I needed to stay close to the doctors. I had many upcoming appointments, plus Dr. Rice had advised me that they were soon going to perform some reconstructive surgery. I had to rely on my robot talk to ask for help and was often asked to "speak up" or repeat myself. That's easy for you to say, I'd gripe to myself.

Waiting for reconstructive surgery, I had no desire to go out in public. It gave me plenty of time to mope over times gone by, both happy and unhappy: the guys I used to hang around with smoking and drinking, the broken romances, some of which really hurt. Before the string of girlfriends, there had even been an early marriage that produced children I barely saw. But I also began thinking of healing in a positive way. I knew that if I stayed cooped up ruminating, I would never develop any courage. I had no way to hide my defects; there was a tube sticking out of my neck and my voice certainly was not my own. In healing, hiding wasn't an option.

Chapter XVII

The Final Fade Out

My old friend Skip and a few loyal members from AA quickly and efficiently moved my belongings to a trailer park in Riverside. The move was a reversal in my expected quality of living. Although my buddy Ray had donated the trailer for my use free of charge, it was musty and run down. Parked amid the squabbles of questionable residents and a landscape of squalor, the trailer could only be described as a place where I stayed alive.

For perhaps the first time in my life I had no one to rescue me, no one to hang onto, no warm hand to hold. Growing up as an only child, my mom and dad provided me with everything I needed. Even after dad died, mom kept me afloat until I marched into marriage with Arlene. That unhappy day when I announced my forthcoming marriage, my mom, poor woman, stammering and hesitatingly told me that I was not their biological son but had been adopted as an infant. I remember the rage I felt as mom tried to explain that even though she was not my biological mother, she had truly loved me and had treated me in every sense as her son. The puzzling 'distance' I'd felt from her and dad at times during my childhood were suddenly explained; the empty feeling of being alone no longer a mystery. I blamed them for my excessive drinking and smoking and allowed this new piece of family history to confirm their 'betrayal.'

Realizing the misery I had put mom through during this difficult period, I had sought her out and made amends: none too soon, for she died shortly thereafter. Parked in the trailer, I allowed myself the agony of thinking about how I had taken for granted the efforts my dad put into his rental houses which eventually provided the only sustenance for mom. My only income now was the rent coming in from the house mom had left to me.

Financial success had come to me early. Arlene's father had an extensive distribution franchise for the L.A. Times, and in this busy, lucrative business, he found a niche for me. Success, pride and the quest for money soon found a soft spot in my character. I began spending a lot of time in dingy Anaheim bars. Inevitably, my attentions became more directed toward my own pleasure rather than to looking after my business, and my wife and children. As though Justice herself had taken a leaf out of my book, success was short lived and lost to me along with the sad end to my first marriage. I denied my condition and defended my way of life until Arlene left me, taking my four daughters with her.

Inexorably both addictive smoking and compulsive drinking became uppermost in my daily routine; the one filling my lungs with tar and slowly causing massive damage to my larynx, the other insidiously invading my intellect and leading me like a lamb to the slaughter. My marriage over, I recklessly pursued my indulgence, paying little attention to all the signs of looming disaster. I cast around for a new partner who would understand who I really was and treat me in a manner befitting my opulence and style.

The woods were full of them, and pretty soon I had a sweet woman hanging on my arm who knew a wrinkle or more than I about getting the "best" out of life. She introduced me to cocaine. In a world which had become unrecognizable, we were married and divorced in an unproductive, unremarkable space of time. Forging ahead, I kept a drink in one hand, a cigarette in the other. It would take me decades to understand the lethal nature of that combination.

The second divorce did not deter me from my mad pursuit of the unattainable, and my life continued along a track designed to kill me. The life I voted for myself, self-destructive though it was, was aided and abetted by the persuasive, impulsive powers of addiction.

Self-loathing, if handled carefully and therapeutically, can be a life-saver. After a while I began to recognize that the person that lived in my skin was some kind of a caricature of me; a person I despised. I actually started listening, carefully, to people concerned about my drinking. I decided that my drinking was going to kill me or put me in prison or into an insane asylum. It was time.

The fellowship of Alcoholics Anonymous became a haunt of mine and thus my savior. It came with only a small set back – nearly everyone in AA smoked in those days! But at least I was dealing with one addiction.

Firmly pointed to recovery from alcoholism, I found myself drawn to California's north state, a place I'd visited often. Perhaps it was just a geographical pull, but I knew that I had to move out of southern California. After packing as much as I could into my El Camino, I took I-5 north and sent the remains of my belongings by carrier.

Redding became my home. With Mount Lassen to the northeast and the mystic snowcapped monument of Mount Shasta dead ahead, there is no mistaking the pull of the Cascade, Siskyou, and Trinity mountains. I found a neat house, rented it and lived comfortably attending AA each evening and building a new pin-striping business.

I visited southern California occasionally. Mutual friends introduced me to Jeannie, and she became my long-distance love. The relationship with Jeannie had barely started when I noticed a slight change in my voice, or rather a change in the volume of my voice. On a short trip to Los Angeles, Jeannie confirmed my fears – my voice had indeed become noticeably weaker. I then recognized that my energy level was down and I had a niggly, raw feeling in my throat. Once back home in Redding, I began to focus on the discomfort in my throat until it became a monstrous fear.

With the nimbleness of trained fingers, the ENT doctor soon found the spot in my neck. After a visual examination of my throat he announced the apparent return of cancer in a lymph node. A biopsy confirmed my worst fears.

"You've had your full exposure to radiation, George," he told me after I had glibly reminded him that radiation had done the job last time. "It's no longer an option. We'll have to perform throat surgery. Only then will we know how invasive the cancer is and we may have to perform a laryngectomy."

The full fury of my self-recrimination and all my fears combined to set my mind in panic as I left the doctor's office. Yes, I had been smoking, but everything looked okay. Had I done this to myself? Perhaps this doctor was wrong. There was a chance! I would get a second opinion. I was determined to get the best care, as if I were president. I would go back to southern California and see what the doctors down there had to say.

I'd actually beaten cancer – and here it was back again.

Chapter XVIII

Diagnosis No. 2 – Cancer

When sitting in the waiting room of Riverside Hospital's leading head and neck surgeon, I heard a strange sounding voice behind me. Slouched unhappily in my chair, my focus was on my throat and the difficulty I was experiencing swallowing. Then I heard the noise again and I had to find out from whom it came.

A few rows behind me sat a middle-aged black man with his wife. I suspected that the voice was his. As I watched, his wife leaned over and said something to him. In reply, he placed his thumb at the base of his throat and I heard him speak in that gravelly voice. When he removed his hand, I saw that there was a patch where his thumb had been and wondered if he had had a laryngectomy. If so, how come he was talking?

Dr. Petty conducted a thorough examination of my throat and agreed with the findings of the doctor in Redding. It was to be surgery - or death. My odds on survival were fifty-fifty. I may have brought it to the attention of a doctor soon enough, for only those whose tumors are caught early have the best chance for survival.

Christmas was just around the corner. I simply couldn't face getting a stoma for Christmas. In desperation, I asked the surgeon to put the surgery off until after the season. He reluctantly agreed but advised that further delay could be very detrimental to a satisfactory result.

I returned to Redding in a very troubled state of mind. My business was doing okay but I couldn't get too excited about it. With surgery now scheduled for January, all I could do was focus on my unhappy circumstances.

January rolled around and I made my way back to Riverside only to discover that some blood stored in the blood bank had been contaminated with HIV. I would have to bank my own blood to prepare for surgery. In my weakened condition, I was only capable of giving one unit every other week. As the weeks dragged by, I relied on painkillers and Jeannie's good nature to sooth my savaged soul.

With the last unit of my own blood banked, I had my final interview with the surgeons who would perform the operation. They told me about the hole I would have in my throat and the subsequent stoma; they also told me about the risk of infection.

"You'll most likely be able to use an electro-larynx to communicate with people. Lousy device, but it works," they told me.

"What about that guy I saw in your waiting room?" I asked. He had some device which allowed him to talk when he depressed his throat. I saw him here a couple of months back."

They explained that this man had been fitted with a Blom-Singer valve. The valve was inserted in the stoma and allowed regulated amounts of air to be pushed up from the trachea to the mouth using the throat muscles. I had witnessed the other patient controlling the amount of air drawn in through the stoma by varying pressure on the valve with his thumb. Once the air reached the mouth, the noise that came from the laryngectomee was as close to a normal sounding voice as one could get.

Later that week I met the other patient, Dave, at a local Denny's restaurant. With my fast fading voice I spoke with Dave for hours. I was thrilled to know that this man had gone through what I was about to go through - and was able to talk. It gave me a huge boost of self-confidence, which, at the thought of losing my voice, was rapidly dwindling. I was looking for some kind of normalcy in a life where one of my first line communicators, my voice, would be seriously hindered. I had gained a couple of new heroes – Doctors Blom and Singer.

The day before my surgery, Dr. Petty's colleague, Dr. Rice, patiently and exactly told me about the upcoming procedure.

"We know pretty well how large the tumor is, George, but we will not know precisely what we are dealing with until we see how it is lying in respect to the lymph. We'll locate it, biopsy, cut and biopsy until there is no further evidence of cancer cells. What I am telling you is that we have no exact measurements of how far we may be obliged to go. We can't be certain how far the cancer has spread."

I nodded wearily. My brain, fuzzy with pain meds as it was, got the message this doctor of medicine was giving me.

Dr. Rice continued for a few minutes longer. "We have had cases similar to yours where the cancer has invaded the breastplate, and in certain cases we've had to remove the breastplate. We just don't know, yet, but we'll certainly do everything we can to remove all the cancer."

Now he had my complete attention. I imagined more, perhaps, than I really knew, but in my sickened state of mind all I wanted was to get the misery over with. God was a relatively new player in my life; I didn't know too much about Him. But AA had taught me that there was someone in my life greater than I, with more power than I, and that He would help.

The discomfort in my throat had progressed to almost unbearable pain and massive amounts of painkillers hardly did the job. I was vomiting constantly and I had lost a lot of weight. On the day I checked in for surgery I was so shaky and feeble that Jeannie had to half-carry me into the waiting room. No seats were available as a crowd of cancer patients waited their turn. I slid down the wall to seat myself on the floor. I watched Jeannie handle my check-in, talking with a kindly faced nurse.

Pre-op ministrations were welcome on that day. Whatever they gave me as a tranquilizer did its work and my painful world, both physical and mental, began to fade until the bright surgery arc lamps were shining in my eyes. It became as quiet and painless as the tomb as the anesthesiologist gazed at me dispassionately over his face mask.

Chapter XIX

That's Easy for You to Say

Tucked away in the stuffy trailer, I was a far different man than the one who had checked into Riverside Hospital for surgery, and vastly different than the one who had taken radiation at Loma Linda. My looks had changed, my voice had certainly changed, but the greatest and by far the most important adjustment was my general attitude to other people and life itself. The cocky George of my youth was permanently retired.

I marked time watching the other trailer park residents shuffle by, glassy-eyed, quite clearly under the influence of whatever substance they had put into their bodies. I came into their line of sight but they didn't see me, and that was the way I wanted it. My electro-larynx became old hat, the novelty worn off. I quit carrying it all together. There was no need for it here.

However, I had my heart set on the Blom-Singer valve. The doctors predicted I was a candidate for the valve, but my surgery was so severe I had months of healing ahead before we could explore that option. I also had my heart set on getting out of Ray's trailer.

Between my ex-girlfriend Anne and my last girlfriend Jeannie, I enjoyed a short but sweet romance with Mary Kay. We remained friends after I decided to relocate to Redding. It was a great surprise to see her again during a check-up at Riverside Hospital. She revealed that she was the intake nurse on the day Jeannie checked me in for surgery!

"I didn't recognize you, George," said Mary Kay. "I had to double check when I saw your name on the intake chart." She acknowledged following my progress until I was released from the hospital.

It was in a room rented to me by Mary Kay that I spent a tranquil six months completing surgery check-ups, mastering the electro-larynx and waiting for the Blom-Singer valve. Dr. Rice finally announced that the healing was significant enough to allow for a fitting. I was getting the valve!

Jubilantly I rushed to the hospital. The examination was simple and brief. After cancer surgery, the fitting procedure was a piece of cake. The procedure began with a precise puncture in the thin tissue that divided my esophagus from my trachea. Through this minute hole went the prosthetic valve. The first two didn't quite fit snugly enough. By a process of elimination they found one that fitted to our mutual satisfaction. I was finally able to push enough air into my mouth which enabled me to make a few gurgling sounds. It worked!

The disappointment was minor when I went home that day with a *red robin* in place, rather than the Blom-Singer valve. The hard rubber tube would keep the new puncture open while it healed. The very next week, I met my speech pathologist, Karen. With as much hope and expectation as I, she removed the *red robin* and deftly inserted the new valve. Then began her not-so-easy job of trying to explain the complex task of *tracheoesophageal* speech.

For the umpteenth time I heard her say, "Try again, George. Don't forget to regulate your breathing. This is like Talk-Yoga." I had to remember that my breathing could no longer be random, as it had been for the past many years. If I wished to say something, I had to regulate my breathing so that the right amount of air came from my lungs, past my valve, and into my mouth where it was compressed into intelligible speech patterns.

At last I sent a hiccup of "hello" through my lips. I was exhausted, but ready to learn more as Karen taught me how to hygienically maintain my valve and replace it with a fresh one each month.

My last visit to Karen was as dramatic as it was successful. In her inimitable style she breezed into the waiting room. "Good morning, George," she said with a big grin.

With an equally big grin I motioned her to stop where she was, while I placed my thumb to my stoma. Slowly and carefully I replied, "That's easy for you to say."

Her face lit up and in a second she had given me a big hug. We both laughed out loud, hers a musical trill, mine a chattering wheeze. The sound was magic.

Chapter XX

Cutting a Deal with God

A couple of months after being fitted with my Blom-Singer valve, I was sitting at Mary Kay's trying to get into a book. A restlessness began to overwhelm me that evening and I grew fidgety. I couldn't figure out what it was all about. Then it dawned on me: I had to get moving again; working again instead of resting at Mary Kay's house. I had mastered my Blom-Singer valve, popping it in and out like a seasoned wearer of contact lenses. I kept my stoma and the valve in good condition as instructed. There was nothing to hold me in southern California but my own lethargy. Thoughts of Redding and the friends I had up there finally made up my mind for me.

Once again I packed my 1971 El Camino and started up Interstate 5 toward Sacramento and Redding. I had qualms about leaving Mary Kay and the treasured friendship we shared. But I had no qualms about leaving Riverside until I was two thirds of the way home. It was then that the voices of logical doubt began to whisper in my ear. *You are going back to Redding empty handed. You haven't got a dime to your name. Do you think that you'll be able to break back into the car-striping business? What are you thinking, George; you are supposed to be sober!*

The voices continued as I drove through the night and neared Redding. As I pulled off the highway I realized that I was facing the reconstruction of the rest of my life. Could I do it? There and then I cut a new deal with God. It went something like this: *You know that I am scared to death about trying to resurrect my old business, and that I really don't want to go into the dealers talking like this. So, if you'll steer me through this mess, I'll do anything you want me to in return. I'll be really open with you. Just point me in the right direction. I'm ready to give back, to help people avoid ending up like me. I'll work with kids, just line them up and I'll do the work.*

As I finished making my deal, I felt a new calmness, and I knew that everything was going to be alright. I stopped off at my Redding rental house and spent the night with friends who had sublet it. Next day, I counted out the rest of what money I had and rented a small house on the other side of town. I quietly moved in and waited for further instructions. I had taken my deal with God seriously knowing that the opportunity to save lives, or at least make them better, awaited me.

Chapter XXI

Coming to Life

Soon after my arrival in Redding, my first venture into society came in the form of scouring the auto dealers in an attempt to sell my pin-striping expertise. Not only was I feeling like the odd man out trying to recapture some of his former glory, but there was also a certain amount of paranoia wrapped up in my approach. I knew that in the car selling industry there is a lot of cigarette smoking, and my fear was that my raspy voice, a dead giveaway for a man who has had a laryngectomy, would turn them off. Fortunately for me, my financial picture was so bleak that I continued to canvas.

I tried to hide my stoma with a button-up shirt, but my voice was my downfall. I remembered Charlie, a man with whom I had worked and who ran three car lots. I went to see him – and hit the jackpot.

After his initial curiosity about my present condition, we got down to business.

"You're a good striper, George," he said, "and we've missed you around here. Take a look around the lot, make an inventory of what you'll need and we can take it from there."

Clipboard in hand and walking on cloud nine, I wandered through the lot identifying cars that needed attention and a list of the product I would need. I talked to salesmen on the lot, some of whom I already knew and others meeting me for the first time. I told many of them about my surgery and how lucky I was to be alive, but they were only mildly curious and the subject was left where it belonged – in my consciousness not theirs. Returning to Charlie an hour later with a long list of needs, I was delighted to have him direct me to work on the same day. I walked off that lot in the evening with $1,500 in my pocket. Within days I had my business up and running. It was called "The Finishing Touch." Triumph and gratitude were my two main emotions for many days. I had quelled much of my initial fear of not being able to find work because of my laryngectomy, and was sure that the man upstairs was responsible for leading me to the right place. Was my deal with God going to pay off? I would soon find out.

One day shortly after my triumphant return to business I sat, coffee in hand, browsing through the classifieds when one ad caught my attention. The American Cancer Society was looking for volunteer drivers to shuttle patients to medical appointments. The only requirement was insurance and a valid drivers' license. I had both; I also had the inclination and a fair amount of free time.

That afternoon I met Bob Logan, manager of the ACS field office; a man with boundless energy and a passion for saving lives. His sparkling blue eyes and infectious grin welcomed me to the team of volunteers. After a short interview wherein he learned of my cancer history, he encouraged me to articulate my experiences: "You know, George, you have an extremely powerful message to give."

During the following year, my free time was spent ferrying cancer patients to and from treatment appointments. I felt humbled to be able to do it and reminded myself many times that I could well have been one of my passengers. I had to admit to myself that I was finally learning some lessons about my fellow human beings. The fellowship of Alcoholics Anonymous had been the first door of opportunity through which I had walked. The Cancer Society was the second. I was a willing student and I had taken the first two opportunities to improve my relationship with God and my fellow human being.

During this period of my life I continued to return to UCLA Medical Center for my own personal medical checks-up. I became a firm and constant attendee at AA meetings and sponsored some younger members who wished to extend their acquaintance with sobriety. After declaring that there would never be another woman in my life, I found Sandra, a former model, who took the wind out of my sails. She turned out to be good company and just what I needed to boost my burgeoning self-confidence. As a matter of fact I had dated several ladies since my return to Redding; Sandra happened to be the most desirable.

Susanville, in Lassen County, was about one hundred and forty miles east of Redding. It became my first out-of-town business venture with The Finishing Touch. Even though my contacts up there in the high country were relatively few, they were pleasant. But the most pleasure I got out of Susanville was the journey there and back. Out through the lush grasslands of Millville and up into the foothills I'd climb, driving through the majestic pines and towering Sierra Nevada mountains until I reached the high desert. On practically deserted, picturesque roads, it became a magical tour.

One afternoon on my way back from Susanville, I decided to break up the drive and do some exploring. I picked Long Hay Flat Road and turned off. The road soon became gravel roadways leading to several widely spaced log cabins and mobile homes, all deep in the lush foliage bounded by a brilliant creek. Curiosity and the birth of an idea stopped me and I decided to get a closer look at these forest-bound homes. My house in Redding suddenly became dull and not the cozy place I once knew. I pulled up in front of a mobile home with a For Sale sign perched out front.

An older man came out to greet me. "Can I help you?" he asked.

"Yeah," I said, standing on his porch steps. "I saw your 'For Sale' sign. I might be interested. Would you tell me about the place?"

He didn't mind at all but it soon became clear that the price he wanted was far beyond anything I could come up with. My spirits sank as fast as they had risen.

"You know," the older man went on, "there's a place up the road across the bridge. It's been for sale some time now, but I don't think he's sold it. Actually we haven't seen the owner for some time."

I got directions, turned my car around and headed for the old one-lane bridge. Turning left on Oak Lane, I saw the weathered For Sale sign and turned into a narrow rutted road and rolled toward a weather-beaten, clapboard sided shack, the deck of which partially encircled a green oak. I grew excited as I walked around the place. I belong here, an inner voice cried. Yes, I'm going to make this place my own, ferns, saplings, Douglas firs, spruce, and all. I noticed with the thrill of a townsperson, the deer hoof prints in the dirt outside the deck.

Within thirty days, the little cabin on Bailey Creek was mine. The $60,000 deal was a great relief for the old owner, a bargain for me, and a hair-cut and shave for my new house. Sandra and I stayed together for some years. Later she told me that she initially thought I had bought the place to die in, whereas I had actually bought it to start living in.

Chapter XXII

Where Snow and Sundays Collide

I remember well those early days of an unnamed freedom – freedom from cancer itself, and the worries thereof. The sharpest and most enjoyable days would surely be those winter weekends spent in the cabin, daring the weather to strand us all with a heavier snowfall than anticipated. If I had a free weekend, a group of us would gather at my Bailey Creek cabin and laugh at the delights of being snug, safe and warm while snow fell silently, cloaking the firs and leafless trees with garlands of frozen particles.

"Hey, George" someone would yell, "the TV screen's getting all snowy. Time to clean the dish off."

Donning my down coat and boots, stout enough to take me to the arctic circle and back, I would step outside with broom in hand and take exaggerated ponderous steps toward the big concave antenna. Attacking it as though I were a Minuteman, the snow would fly in all directions until I heard the cheers from inside the cabin telling me that the picture had reappeared.

I'd dip back through my deep footsteps in the snow, holding the broom overhead for balance. It wouldn't be long before the snow won out and, again, I'd make the trek to the satellite dish. This was a ritual in which I gladly participated whenever snows and Sundays collided. Stamping snow from my boots and peeling icy gloves from my hands, my heroic re-entry into the warmth and friendship was enough to make snowy football Sundays a truly memorable event.

Chapter XXIII

Willingly Up a Creek

My life at Bailey Creek was all about the process; the spiritual process of rejoining the human race: refurbishing my tattered emotions, readjusting an oversized ego, and learning something about humility. Thanking the God of my understanding for restoring my body to a reasonable semblance of what it once was and learning to overcome some of the deficiencies with which the surgery had left me. In short, I was mending.

Working on the physical challenge of restoring the Bailey Creek cabin to some of its former glory got rid of some of the worthlessness I had accumulated during the years prior to getting sober. I was dedicated to repairing broken wood and replacing rotten timbers that brought me face to face with the glint of silver I had seen so many years ago lying in a hospital bed in southern California. I filled ruts in the road so that my polished El Camino would not sustain major damage, and trimmed vegetation so that spring would bring forth new life to encourage my new life.

In late September my new abode was ready to be lived in. With a few friends and a large U-Haul we packed all my belongings and brought them up the hill to Bailey Creek. Had I thought about the true significance of this event in any light other than that of a great, positive adventure, I would surely have scared myself to death. From city mouse to raccoon in one fell swoop: from the big city lights and noise, to the shady silence of the forest. The furniture went where it fitted, and when it didn't fit it went on the porch.

While we unpacked and set up, joshed and kidded, my thoughts never strayed from the present, but later, it was a different story.

Dusk was settling in and we called it a day. With hugs and farewells, the crew piled into the truck and disappeared down Oak Lane toward the bridge, leaving behind an unsure, exhausted city boy.

I stood for a while trying to drink in the grandeur as I had imagined it, but a certain fear overtook me and I wondered if I had taken leave of my senses. Why had I come all the way into the mountains to live? In the descending dusk, animals were busy doing what animals do before the winter hits them. I had simply joined them, and my spirits went up a notch. Turning my back on the fears, I came inside and planned some activities for the coming weeks. At last, exhausted, I unrolled my sleeping bag and slept.

Each new day after that became more and more appealing. I became entranced by the simple beauty of Bailey Creek and its other inhabitants. Each day was a feast unto itself. Sometimes I'd do nothing but hang around the cabin doing small chores. On others I would take long walks on the logging tracks that interwove Lassen forest. On yet other occasions, I hewed and stacked five cords of pine for my woodstove, the only form of heat available.

Sandra, who stayed in the city, donated large pieces of a slightly worn carpet she had replaced with a new one. Joy of joys, to walk around my cabin and feel the pile between my toes!

Once in a while I invited friends out to show off my refurbished cabin – new bathroom, new kitchen – but I was no longer in the mood for big parties. My purpose up here was to develop my character and tune my spirit. I commuted into town for business and attended as many AA meetings as I could squeeze in.

Living as I did, I came to realize early that 'living' was not a daily chore but a gift to us to fabricate the best of every hour and minute of every day. I reflected on the manner in which I had wasted my life wantonly and the price I had paid so far. I was resolved not to take that path again. I changed my belief system.

Christmas brought its own wonders up at Bailey Creek. Huge snowfalls arrived and the incredible beauty that accompanies these winter phenomena. The serenity and the majesty were almost indescribable. I found that I began to have faith; faith in my fellow human being, faith in God, but most importantly, faith in myself.

Chapter XXIV

Listening to the Wilderness

I had always loved the mountains, and living in this glady nook in the forest was a dream come true. I spent long, leisurely hours at my self-hewn picnic table placed in a hideaway by the creek. In my little wild alcove, I allowed my mind to drift downstream with the swift flowing current as it meandered its way past Lassen, down into the Sacramento Valley on its way to the ocean.

Weather permitting, coffee on the deck started my day. I took note of the squirrel and blue jay activity, by far the busiest and most industrious of my neighbors. Once in a while I would glimpse a red fox drinking from an eddy in the creek.

One morning, mug in hand, I went over to the smaller, empty cabin next to mine and sat on the edge of the deck drinking in the morning beauty. Suddenly a loud *SNAP* brought my attention to a grove of manzanita bushes. A few feet from my startled face, I found myself gazing in awe at the large antlered head of a buck. What a grand sight! Bright eyed, holding his five point rack quite still, we looked at each other. Soon he was joined by two tawny does. They, too, stopped in their tracks and gazed at me with apprehension.

Ever so slowly I managed to lower my coffee mug to the deck and with equal stealth, bring my hand up to my neck. Pressing the air up past my throat muscles, I told the animal in a low husky voice, "I'm not going to hurt you. Everything is going to be okay."

Our eyes were locked in the moment. "You have nothing to fear from me," I said, and at that moment this magnificent beast effortlessly about-faced and bounded away. The two does followed suit. This magic moment put the wonder and beauty of nature in true perspective making DSL and cell phones seem archaic.

During the summer months I explored the numerous trails that criss-crossed through the forest, and became as familiar with some of them as I had with the streets of Fullerton. Some of the mysteries of the uncivilized world were also revealed. Kicking the stump of a rotting tree, for instance, I would see who lived in those dark, damp worlds – salamanders, centipedes and slaters – and large mountain ants, leviathan of industry in their own small world. I learned to recognize wild flowers; lupines, Indian flame, and to beware of poison oak, that attractive but irritating shrub that can turn your life into a misery. It seemed that I couldn't get enough of the enchanting scenery; the slant of sunlight through fir trees and the way the sun brought brilliance to a patch of blackberry bushes or elderberries.

When the snow lay feet deep on the trails and logging roads that I'd gaily trodden during the high country summer, I zoomed over them at high speed on my snowmobile. On those trails I took in the bright, blinding sunshine, and, when I shut off the engine, I marveled at the utter silence that enveloped the landscape. It was interrupted only by the slithering *crump* as snow, collected on the boughs, fell to the ground under the sun's warmth. It became more exciting, of course, during less clement weather when the wind moaned or tore through the bare branches telling tales of past wanderers and emigrants, and their hardships. I likened it to eavesdropping on the wilderness which, by its very nature, leaves visible signs of man's trek through its untamed preserves, but also recounts the adventurous passages of the interlopers.

It was here that I learned the elements of meditation, spending extending periods of time, from minutes to hours, listening to my inner voices; understanding where they came from; being honest with my reviews. I encountered resentment, revenge and laziness. It took quite some time to learn to forgive; that journey is a continuing one and will take me to the end of my days.

My journey started at Bailey Creek and continued through the four seasons of each year. I grasped on to the new beginning; the journey continues!

Chapter XXV

Farewell to Bailey Creek

During the time I spent at Bailey Creek, I dutifully commuted into town every day of the week, working at the car lots; earning my living. I did, however, reserve every weekend for myself and my two dogs, Shasta and Ashley. Friday evening would see us on the road to Bailey Creek. I cherished every hour I spent in my cabin, and even though I loved my AA groups and the many friends I had made in this somewhat quaint northern town, a feeling of relief would suck the worry out of me and fill my soul with the joyous anticipation of reaching my hermitage. I nested in for my reward – peace, quiet and the sounds of nature. I found that the reverse emotions were present when I drove back to Redding on Monday morning. A niggling anxiety would gnaw at my serenity and the clarity of my mind dimmed with the worldly clutter of the job, relationships and the muddle of town.

Why did it all have to change? The spring of 1998 brought record rainfall; near ninety inches fell during the season. It caused massive flooding county wide and changed Bailey Creek into a savage torrent of uncontrolled water. The clayey earth, baked hard during six months of almost tropical sun, was unable to absorb any of the heavy rains, and it therefore ran wild into ditches, creeks and streams filling the Sacramento River to dangerous levels. During one particular storm, my own meandering creek became a raging torrent within a few hours, overflowing its niggardly banks and becoming a sizeable confluence.

The noise of heavy rain on the roof wakened me. I lay for a few moments luxuriating in the warmth of my bed. When I finally got up and looked out of the window, I was alarmed to see that Bailey Creek, no longer a hidden brook, was roaring just a few yards from my cabin. Dressing quickly, I hurried up the road to find out how my neighbor, Bill, had fared and was relieved to find the frail eighty year old safe and sound. Several of the local inhabitants joined me as I followed the path of "our river" toward the main highway. Oak Street Bridge, over which I drove to get to my place, appeared to be under several feet of water. What now? Was this a place where I could safely stay year round? Might next year's rains sweep my only residence into the Sacramento River?

Perhaps I'd had my fill of rural life; in any event I decided to leave my retreat and rejoin the rest of the world. With a surprising upsurge of spiritual strength, I put the cabin on the market just as soon as the weather had stabilized and Bailey Creek had returned to its normal size, albeit having left signs of its destructive path; wider banks and felled trees.

As though I had been rejuvenated, I walked away from Bailey Creek looking at my future and prospects of things to come as through a new pair of glasses. Life in the wilderness had enabled me to place myself realistically in the slot into which I fitted in this universe of ours. My life had actually been wrapped in a lovely silver lining; it felt good to be alive, not just one day a week, but every day. Time to give back to those who had seen me through the toughest times. I have to tell you that I arrived back in Redding with a far lighter load than the day, three years prior, that I'd left.

Chapter XXVI

Something to Give

"When the student is ready and willing, a teacher will appear." I heard that proverb earlier in my life, and understood it so thoroughly that I repeated it to many people over the years. When I was ready to learn about and accept physical healing, I was presented with an array of fine physicians, surgeons and therapists. I shall never forget and be forever grateful to Doctors Petty and Rice and all the attending medical professionals who carved and stitched my body back together again. A masterful job was done that damaged little but my ego.

During my emotional downtime, when the mental agony of low self esteem, worthlessness and alcoholism needed more than cursory attendance, Alcoholics Anonymous came to the rescue and gave me sufficient spiritual fiber to learn how to engage in self-healing at Bailey Creek. Through the selfless acts of many friends, including those in AA, I learned gratitude and found out how to give back, in part, through Bob Logan of The American Cancer Society. My connection to ACS changed my future forever. I shall never forget being a volunteer driver, taking those patients back to their homes after they received chemotherapy, and seeing fear and apprehension in their faces. I knew that some of them I might never see again, but

I knew that even just a touch of the hand and a gentle smile could take the edge off their worry.

One day shortly after I returned to Redding, Bob called on me with a new and daunting request. He told me that a local high school teacher had contacted him and asked him if he knew anyone who might speak to teenagers as part of a Tobacco Use Prevention Education Program. Looking at me expectantly over the tops of his glasses, he asked, "How about it?"

I stopped in my tracks. I was not a public speaker and might freeze up in front of the whole school! "You're a survivor, George, not a teacher or politician; you are better than anyone to tell the truth about a popular drug that is killing millions."

I said I would do it, and cursed myself all the way home for being a weak- kneed fool.

It was the Great American Smokeout, the big day to quit smoking, when I stood with Bob in the high school corridor feeling speechless and confused. I was about to get up in front of a room full of young men and women preparing to graduate from Enterprise High School. What was I going to tell them? How would I present my case?

Bob was there to calm my jangling nerves. "You'll do fine," he said and slapped me on the back. Twenty-eight heads swiveled toward me as I entered the classroom. The rustle of books and paper slowly quieted as the teacher told her students to put their work away. Greeting me with a smile, she shook my hand and introduced me to her class as a "special guest." A sea of inquisitive faces gazed at me. The teacher, now sitting with her class, looked at me and raised her eyebrows. I was on.

"My name is George Willets," I began, "and I'm the poster boy for what you don't want to do when you graduate from school." My thumb hovered over my stoma patch before I continued with my talk. To my relief and surprise, there were no snickers, just the concentrated gaze of twenty-eight pairs of wide eyes. I told them all about my long relationship with tobacco and how quickly I became addicted to it. I told them, without any frills, how it led to cancer, about my close call with death from that disease, and receiving a laryngectomy that radically altered my life. Eventually, I demonstrated my old electro-larynx to let them know how it sounded.

"How would you like this machine to be the only way you could talk?" I asked them in that monotonous robotic sound. The room filled with interested murmurs. "Imagine being in a restaurant, or on a date. That would really catch people's attention." There were giggles. "…or in a movie theatre!" I smiled broadly and the whole class smiled with me – and relaxed.

When I asked for volunteers to come up and try the electro-larynx, the show of hands was slight. In time, that would change. But on that day, I was delighted at the few who came up and tried their hands at using the E-L. They tried, but no sound could they produce. "That's easy for you to say," I teased the last volunteer.

"Pretty funny isn't it?" I asked them, but changed my tone when I followed up with, "but I guarantee that it wouldn't be so funny if you had to speak like this."

That first engagement with Enterprise High convinced me that I didn't have the right to withhold information that could change the lives of many children. What I had to share, not only with children, but with the rest of the smoking world, was vital in the prevention of addiction to nicotine. The information I had could save lives from that deadliest of all diseases, cancer.

Public speaking as a laryngectomee…that was the course I decided to take!

Chapter XXVII

Presenting George Willets

I later considered that my talks at Enterprise High School were graduate courses in giving. On the first day, I left that seat of learning feeling joyous with a certain urge to give more. Even though I knew it would be difficult to explain to a classroom of school children the nature and power of addiction, and that the man talking to them, the man who was telling them to avoid the hidden dangers of nicotine, had also been addicted, I knew full well that the truth had to come out.

Whatever benefits I bestowed on my audiences, they returned them with big-heartedness. I believed that those children were receiving information vital to their own future, to their health. In such educational talks, I was ever a supporter of the maxim that if only one person benefited from my talk, then the whole thing was well worth it.

With growing self-respect and an increasing sense of self-worth, I started a crusade which would take me near and far into the paths of children who might become victims of the cigarette companies' sly but attractive advertisements. I had to overcome my shyness and get the word out about my activities. My friend Bob became my ambassador. It was he who introduced me to Rebecca, a health educator from Shasta County Public Health, who then called on me to lecture at some of the local public schools. She also loaned me her "tar jar", containing a revolting collection of old burned cigarette stubs, plus a set of heavily nicotine stained teeth.

More than happy to attend these schools and deliver my now fairly well memorized lecture, I found that I was eligible for a small stipend; I was after all, a public speaker. Since I believe that God led me to this job, I found it ironic that He should have found me work as a public speaker especially since I'd quite recently had my larynx excised.

I had never anticipated or expected any payment for my services. So far as I was concerned, I was giving my time and knowledge away. One day, however, the high school district asked me to help them out with a novel prevention program they had instituted. Teenagers who were caught smoking were ordered to attend anti-smoking classes on four successive Saturdays; they asked me to speak and offered me a small remuneration in return for my services.

Rather than rudely reject the school district's offer, I consulted a trusted friend in AA.

He explained that since the school district was already receiving money expressly for tobacco education, the very purpose that I was serving, I should take the money as payment for services rendered. I did so and threw my whole heart and soul into trying to get through to those young people.

Nothing succeeds like success! A short while later while attending to my job in a car lot, I met Stanley, a football coach, who asked me if I would travel to Anderson, a town south of Redding, to present my anti-smoking talks to sixth, seventh and eighth grade youngsters. I readily agreed – and learned another lesson.

For all my energy and enthusiasm, after giving four talks a day on three successive days, both my voice and my energy level suffered. I found it difficult to keep my voice up to an audible level, and by the end of the third day, I was dragging. I had to pace myself. If they were going to pay me, I decided that the quality of my deliveries had better be greater than the quantity.

One day I received a call from a woman named Deborah, an ACS volunteer and a person I instantly trusted and liked. She was an active member of the Shasta County Tobacco Education Coalition and worked with the county schools anti-tobacco efforts. I was asked to give the keynote speech at a regional training she was organizing in northern California. The Teens Against Tobacco Conference, as it was called, was a joint effort between the American Cancer Society, the county department of public health and the county office of education.

The Saturday came when a large group of volunteer teenagers representing high schools from nine counties were brought to the conference in Redding. I watched the Red Lion ballroom fill up with a mixture of fear, pride and gratitude. Deborah stayed by my side, as did Bob Logan, Rebecca from Public Health and a junior high media instructor, Alan. I learned that Alan was directing his students in making tobacco-related commercials. It was exciting when he asked me to join them for an interview.

I believe that my presentation was a huge success in spite of my 'butterflies.' As I listened to Deborah give the opening talk to the crowd of over one hundred teens, the butterflies seemed to be absorbed into the importance of the occasion.

That was the start of an enduring friendship and alliance with Deborah. After that weekend, she approached me for another constructive meeting with a view to finding out where I would like to go with my lectures; would I like to expand the topic? Her aim was to encourage more teenagers to stay tobacco-free or to quit smoking. Her hope for them involved my voice of experience.

About a month later she had organized a tour of Shasta County schools. Later she told me how impressed she was, not only with my presentation but with the way the youngsters had listened to my delivery with such attention. She told me, "You have a rare gift, George. I am privileged to be part of it."

As Deborah and I continued to work together, she revealed her ambition to write a book and her growing interest in using my story as the theme. She shared my passion for getting the word out to youth about the lure of tobacco, its hidden danger and the ravages, including death, that would come with its continued use. Deborah became the stitching in my silver lining.

Chapter XXVIII

As Good As It Gets

Things were going my way. I had my pin striping business: not millions of dollars but enough to keep me comfortable. My relatively new venture, and certainly my most exciting one, lecturing to teenagers on the dangers of smoking, seemed to be gathering momentum, the force of which I would soon discover.

On a winter morning, I received a call from the Harrison County Medical Society Alliance in West Virginia. They wanted me to do a tour of their high schools! They were inviting me to talk to students about the subject that had become near and dear to me - the dangers of smoking. Being the kind of person I am, my 'committee' immediately went to work. *George, oh George, this is too big for you. We know you really are flattered and would love to go, but . . . the job is in West Virginia; the other side of the world. It's too far . . . too big, and anyway you're not good enough for it.* All of this filtered through my mind while the Medical Society was waiting at the other end of the line.

Dispelling the fear and worthlessness that had flooded my mind, I allowed the new spirit in me, the real me, to tell them that I'd be delighted.

Deborah, with her natural efficiency and attention to detail, made flawless travel arrangements at the California end and Delia, from the Medical Society, turned out to be equally detailed and a grand chauffeur and guide at the West Virginia end.

I landed in Pittsburg, Pennsylvania and drove to Clarksburg, West Virginia in a little rental car. I enjoyed the change of scenery on the one hundred mile drive but worried about the forthcoming lectures. Would I ever stop fretting about my performance?

Delia met me at the Holiday Inn, where I'd managed to get a few hours sleep the night before. She greeted me as though I were a Hollywood actor or returning hero, and treated me with all the southern hospitality I'd heard so much about. She was the personification of charm. Driving me from school to school each day and introducing me with great courtesy to hundreds of young people was an experience I shall never forget.

I learned that in West Virginia many households are run on tobacco workers' salaries. It's a big industry; about twenty-seven percent of the adults smoke - making it the state with the third highest smoking rate in the nation. Smoking-related job absentee rates were costing the state two billion dollars each year. When I got on stage to speak about the hazards of smoking, the final message of course being, *give it up*, I wondered how many kids in the audience lived in families supported by the tobacco industry? I expected that there would be quite a few and wondered what kind of reception I might receive, if not vocally, then by hostile thoughts?

Standing before the empty bleachers, I stopped my pre-speech reverie and, going back a few years, tried to put myself in the teens' position. Many of them were probably already on the way to nicotine addiction, and if they were of addictive natures, from addictive genes, they might well be on the deadly path of addiction to drugs and alcohol, like I was as a young man. Those distant days were the "high" days. I was on top of the world, or thought I was, so why would these kids not be in a similar place? How could I get a message to them that smoking and drinking are not necessary parts of our lives and that without either we would live healthier and longer lives? Without being self-piteous, could I get them to realize that if they were to avoid these drugs, for nicotine is as surely a drug as heroin, they would not end up like me?

Soon the bleachers were full and Delia, all charm, introduced me. A burst of applause was partially, playfully ignored by me. I walked to the end of the stage and cupped my ear as though I hadn't heard them. The roar doubled. I did it again and I had both their interest and attention. I hadn't yet said a word.

The series of talks in West Virginia was a great success, although it taxed me physically and just about took my voice away. Despite the challenge, three talks a day at three different schools for a week was exhilarating in so many ways. The youngsters thronged around me. They wanted to assure me that they had heard me. They wanted to tell me about how much their parents smoked; how much they themselves smoked and were vowing to quit.

I returned to California from the rainy east coast, surfing along on my highest high. I knew I had connected with those kids and, best of all, I had learned a better way to connect with other youngsters. I knew, at last, that I was giving something back in return for the blessings I had received.

Chapter XXIX

End of Story — Or Perhaps the Beginning

I often wondered if my life would have changed had I known more about the evils of tobacco smoking before I lit my first cigarette. Had someone, like myself, come to my school and given talks about the dangers of tobacco smoking, would I have decided not to smoke because I didn't want to become ill and scarred like him? The only logical answer to that supposition and question is, that had I not smoked (or drank) when I was young, I would never have been able to travel around my home state of California and West Virginia, delivering the messages that may have prevented many young men and women from developing cancer, thereby saving their lives. Had it not been me, then who? There may have been someone else as motivated as I, but there *may not* have been. If you believe in a Power greater than yourself, the only conclusion you can draw is that that person had to be me; it was *destined* to be me.

The plain unadulterated facts speak for themselves. I smoked cigarettes and cigars from the age of twelve for the next thirty odd years. As the years went by, my smoking became insatiable. I was not a freak of nature, for everyone smoked; my dad, all my friends, my friends' parents. Huge signs advertised the best cigarettes, the strongest, those with the best taste and those that made you look like a man! And so when I stood before these young people who smoked, I knew where they were coming from.

I remember a young man in one of my audiences who reminded me a bit of myself. Flipping his shaggy hair out of his eyes, he took the microphone during question time. Nervous and embarrassed he didn't know how to say what he wanted to express. Then, in a burst of enlightenment, said, "Yeah! Hey, George, I just wanted to tell you that this assembly was pretty cool." Looking around quickly at his pals, he jerked the microphone back to his mouth and blurted out, "Just wanted to say, you ROCK!"

The entire group erupted in a universal roar. The kids leapt to their feet and started stamping and clapping, a deafening sound on the bleachers. It took me several minutes to quell the noise. I then turned to the brave young man and said, "I don't think you have finished speaking. Continue."

Our hero, dressed in a black "T" shirt, a little more confident now that he'd broken the ice, held the mic up and said, "Yeah, well I smoke, and after today there's no way I am ever goin' to smoke again. You made me see what can happen."

Music to my ears! I'd got one, at least. "That's brave of you to say that in front of this crowd," I replied, "When did you start?

"A few years ago when I was thirteen," he said. "I smoke Marlboro red box, just like you; I mean just like you did."

"Quitting is one of the toughest things you'll ever have to do," I said, "But I know you can do it. I want you to remember me; I'm the poster boy of what not to do. There is absolutely no need for you to quit the way I did – on morphine after throat surgery."

"No way! I don't want to end up like you," said black t-shirt emphatically. Immediately realizing how his retort may have sounded, he blushed deeply and mumbled, "No disrespect."

"None taken," I said. "That's exactly why I'm here today. I don't want you, nor anyone else in this room today, to turn out like I did. Thank you."

I returned the microphone to its stand. What a great day it had been to be a survivor.

Chapter XXX

Living with My Disease – Acceptance

Ever since my days of living quietly at Bailey Creek I had felt the urge to give back to both my fellow humans and to God. Through meditation and the consequent examination of my thoughts and feelings, I was humbled by the benefits I had received through following His path and the twelve steps of Alcoholics Anonymous. I am happy to report that I achieved part of my wish.

I came to believe that young people, just reaching puberty, needed a guide to lead them through some of the worst perils accepted universally by society - smoking and consuming alcohol. I hasten to add that there are smokers and drinkers, probably many millions of them, who have sailed through their lives without a bad day, but there are many millions more who have not, and ended up with cancer of the throat or the lungs or have drunk themselves into asylums, prison or the grave. All human beings are not created physically and genetically equal. There are those of us who have addictive natures nurtured by genes. I came to know that I was such a person.

Help for people like me has been around in one form or another for a century. Earlier on, addictive drinking was considered to be a weakness. Nowadays there are twelve step programs, many thousands of them in most large cities, where dedicated people already on their way to overcoming whatever obsession they have, are willing and ever ready to help the newcomer.

Smoking tobacco, however, falls into a different social stratum. During the fourteenth century, the importation of tobacco leaf received an eager reception in Spain, Portugal and England. The Portuguese made the first cigarette which was both hailed and reviled; on the one hand it was a soothing drug, and on the other its use was a *filthy habit.* In the United States, quite early on in the eighteenth century, nicotine was isolated and proclaimed to be dangerous to one's health.

Large companies such as Liggett & Meyer, Phillip Morris, and Benson & Hedges found the industry too lucrative to be swayed in the direction of moderation and went all out to sell their product to the public by means of appealing advertisements; millions of dollars worth of advertisements. Cigarettes were touted as being friendly, sexy, manly and feminine. The tobacco industry struck at every human frontier.

Finally, certain chemicals infused into tobacco products were disclosed and declared by the Surgeon General of the United States to be so harmful to the human body as to cause cancer. Slowly, the incidence of smoking-related deaths decreased but not for long. Unrelenting, the tobacco industry continued its campaign to engineer advertisements that would lure the population, now including a huge number of teenagers, to smoke. They remain successful despite damning evidence that cigarette tobacco is harmful to one's health. Many, many millions of people, men, women and children around the world, particularly in South East Asia, Europe and Africa, smoke – and die.

For my own part, I learned to serve my experiences straight up during my public talks. Some of my audience members asked, for instance, "How big is the hole in your neck?" or "What happens when you go swimming?" And "What happens when you drink a glass of water?"

My answers were simple and candid. "My stoma is about the size of a nickel. No, I can't go swimming. My lungs and the stoma are connected; three inches of water could drown me. When I drink anything, the liquid goes straight down my esophagus into my stomach." Amid, "Ooh's" and gasps of disgust, or wonder, I often unveiled my stoma. It was best that people got a view of the truth.

Talking about addiction to children was a difficult task. "Why didn't you just stop smoking when you realized the dangers of smoking?" they asked. Talking about obsession, compulsion, and addiction could easily exceed the adolescent limits to absorb the most critical information I had to give. I had to get them to believe me implicitly when I told them that one of the most difficult things they may have to do in their lives is to quit smoking. The road to that goal, of course, is not to start. I talked to them about the pressure, peer pressure, of accepting a cigarette, especially when it may be their first. Being cool is important, but not at the risk of your own life. Tobacco is an equal opportunity destroyer!

I told my audiences that not everyone suffers the same fate as I, but the game you play by throwing this equation into your decision to smoke or not to smoke, is like playing Russian Roulette. I tried to convince young people that the fleeting moments of euphoria afforded by a few puffs on a cigarette are simply not worth the risk of agonizing pain and suffering, surgery, skin grafts and the hope that the cancer will not return. And return it will if the surgeon fails to detect just one cancer cell and leaves it to multiply. Finally, I always told my audiences about the silver lining I discovered in my cancer, the silver lining that embellishes every fine endeavor we set out to accomplish. I asked them to listen carefully to what I shared with them and think of the humiliation experienced with the loss of one's voice to the harsh, tell-tale rasp of an electronic voice such as I demonstrated on the stage.

Cancer may have escorted me to death's door, but that was one door through which I wasn't ready to pass. I hoped my voice, the only one I had left, cast a lasting impression on all who heard it; all who were touched by it. For my own part, I grew to love it, for it kept me in touch with my fellow human being. At last, that was easy for me to say.

***